SHELF LIFE

Shelf Life

ROMANCE, MYSTERY, DRAMA, AND
OTHER PAGE-TURNING ADVENTURES
FROM A YEAR IN A BOOKSTORE

Suzanne Strempek Shea

BEACON PRESS
BOSTON

BEACON PRESS
25 Beacon Street
Boston, Massachusetts 02108-2892
www.beacon.org

Beacon Press books
are published under the auspices of
the Unitarian Universalist Association of Congregations.

09 08 07 06 05   8 7 6 5 4

This book is printed on acid-free paper that meets the uncoated paper
ANSI/NISO specifications for permanence as revised in 1992.

Text design by Isaac Tobin
Composition by Wilsted & Taylor Publishing Services

LIBRARY OF CONGRESS CATALOGING-IN-PUBLICATION DATA

Shea, Suzanne Strempek.
Shelf life : romance, mystery, drama, and other page-turning
adventures from a year in a bookstore / Suzanne Strempek Shea.
p. cm.
ISBN 0-8070-7258-3 (cloth)
ISBN 0-8070-7259-1 (pbk.)
1. Shea, Suzanne Strempek. 2. Edwards Books. 3. Booksellers and
bookselling—Massachusetts—Springfield—Biography. 4.
Bookstores—Massachusetts—Springfield—Employees—Biography. 5.
Authors, American—20th century—Biography. I. Title.

Z473.S43 2004
381'.45002'092—dc22   2003023155

The excerpt from the poem "The Ballyconnell Colours" was used with
the kind permission of Dermot Healy and The Gallery Press, Loughcrew,
Oldcastle, Co. Meath, Ireland, which first published the collection
The Ballyconnell Colours in 1992.

TO FLORA FERRANTI EDWARDS,
who says I can do whatever I want.

AND TO ALL BOOKSELLERS,
whose stock-in-trade makes the rest of us feel just as powerful.

THIS IS WHAT THEY WANT:

Names for babies. Used car prices. Richard Nixon paper dolls. Tips for performing music on stage. Drug contraindications. Alternatives to the typical smoothie. A guide to the chakra system.

The *Playboy* interviews. A source for old-fashioned bulbs used in the kind of old-fashioned radios that run on old-fashioned bulbs. A map of the Northeast Kingdom. Rules of gay etiquette. The recipe for Ring Dings.

Jesus Christ. The Dalai Lama. Scooby Doo. Rules for arena football. Treatment for a sickly koi. Fluency in Urdu. A copy of the Constitution. The route of the Cinque Terre.

They want to find that special someone. To wed that special someone. On a budget. They want to have a child. Or to adopt a child from one of the less popular categories of children available domestically. They want to decorate its nursery in nontoxic materials, to prepare the family pet, to build cribs and toy trains from scratch even though they've never before held a hammer. They want to knit the child booties and hats bearing traditional Aran Isle patterns. To homeschool it, potty train it, teach it French as its first language. In utero. They want to spark its creativity or to investigate whether its surprisingly high level of imagination could mean it is gifted. They want to deal with its invisible friend, its dyslexia, its bullying, its obesity, its teenage nastiness, its decision to quit college after the first three-and-a-half weeks.

They want the step-by-steps—with illustrations, charts, an accompanying CD or DVD, if possible. They want to sail, crochet, bunt, stir-fry, wail on power chords, win at Scrabble, at chess, at bridge, at keno, at craps. They want to stamp, stencil, weave, weld, paint animals on rocks, construct massive front-door wreaths from roadside branches. They want to master their Windows '98, predict the weather, give an unforgettable toast, do their estate planning, their cornrows, their regrouting, their astrological charts. They have digital cameras, snowboards, termites, shih tzus, plastic ray guns from the '50s. Low blood sugar, wrinkles, back pain, osteoporosis, and something they mercifully stop short at describing as "distress down, you know, down there ..." They have anger, paranoia, addiction, loneliness, "the disease to please," and a whole boatload of unmet needs. They will be going through divorce, through the purchase of a first home, through an audit, through menopause, through the Chunnel from England to France and require nonallergenic sleeping locations at each end.

They are pop culture fanatics, eBay regulars, mystery buffs, day-trippers, insomniacs, water gardeners, scholars, children of the '60s, atheists, Red Sox fans. They are self-employed, self-sufficient, newly retired, newly diagnosed, newly literate.

They all have many questions.

And so they come to me.

The image must be forming now. In your mind I morph from faceless keyboard tapper to knowledge-brimming, mountaintop-dwelling goddess of wisdom. Surely I wear flowing robes in a range of sherbety-hued and other-worldly textured fabrics, and my hair cascades to my toes, where animals of the type that normally eat or otherwise have undesirable bad reactions to humans sleep smilingly at my feet, and birds in colors you never knew birds came in right now are flitting and twittering about my throne as without missing a beat I provide all the answers for all the questions.

Surely.

But not quite.

Reality is, I'm a mere human. My garb is off the rack, my hair reaches no farther than mid-spine, and if there is a creature at my feet, it's no one more exotic than ten-dollar Tiny from the Palmer Pound. You'd be right, though, in picturing me as situated somewhere up high. As I dispense all those answers, the chair on which I sit is

a tall stool, and the floor on which the tall stool is placed
is two stories up, but on nowhere grander than the second
level of a half-darkened, half-occupied urban mall. You are
most on target with the last bit of your image of me: I do
indeed have what everyone is seeking.

Because I sell books.

And because there is a book about nearly everything
you would ever want or need to know, on any subject
that might slightly or greatly interest you, I constantly
am asked for my input. I must be honest and admit that
even a tiny fraction of the answers aren't technically in
my brain. Point is, I know where to find them: in Cooking. In Mystery. In Religion. In Psychology. In Parenting
or Sports or African-American or Business. In Mass-
Market Fiction. Trade Fiction. Reference. U.S.A. Travel.
Foreign Travel. Education. If not there, then in Hardcover New Title. New and Recommended. Hobbies.
Humor. Native American. Recovery. History and Political Science. Young Adult. Children's. Health/Diet/Exer-
cise. Classics. Poetry/Reference/Drama. Gothic (formerly
called "Romance"). Or in Fantasy (formerly "Science Fiction," but wouldn't you think that formerly would have
been "Romance"?).

Those are the names of the sections in my bookstore,
Edwards Books, in downtown Springfield, Massachusetts.
OK, it's not really my store. It's Janet's. Janet Edwards's
store. And that's how many people refer to it. They come
up to the cash register carrying exactly what they were
hoping to find and they say, "I knew I could find this at
Janet's." If the possessive makes it sound like the store is

her home, that's not far from the truth if you consider the amount of time she spends there each of the six days the store is open, and often a seventh to tie up loose ends. But the customers call the store Janet's because Janet is the heart, the soul, the furnace from which emanates the warmth, smarts, unflagging energy, and goodwill that, despite the rather hidden location, a ping-ponging economy, and big-box competition, keeps the place alive. I, too, have long called Edwards Books Janet's, in the same way that when I'm headed to the Broadside Bookshop in nearby Northampton, I say I'm going to Bruce's. Bruce MacMillan founded the store, managed the store, simply was the store for its first twenty-seven years. Three years after his death, I still call the Broadside Bruce's. Nothing at all against Roxie and Nancy and Bill—Roxie and Nancy have worked there twenty-four years, Bill twenty-two. They run it now. In my head, though, the store is Bruce's. Just as Edwards is Janet's. And, somehow, in the three years since she reached out and pulled me onto the staff, I feel that a bit of the store has become mine.

So there I am, one or two afternoons a week, working the register, shelving newly arrived titles, creating displays, setting up events, and, of course, answering those many questions—one moment being asked my opinion about which is the better title on the lives of the saints and, the next, if we have the *Kama Sutra*.

Some questions are not as direct. I'm often racking my brain after being given too few clues about just what it is the reader wants so badly.

"I'm looking for a book. I don't know the title. I don't

have the author's name. I know that it's about a woman. A woman in another country. And it's fiction. The cover is red. My neighbor says it's good. Would you have it?"

"I need some books for children who hate to read. My son hates to read. But I want him to read. Do you have any books that a child could read without realizing he was reading?"

"What would you recommend for a flight to California? I'll be sleeping most of the time."

"It's by the author Shurshill—you know, C-H-U-R-C-H-I-L-L. Like the president?"

"This trilogy has only three books. Where's the fourth?"

"I need a story that won't require me to think."

"It's a book by that woman who was on TV the other morning. She wrote something about families. I don't know her name—wait—she might have been on the *Today* show, or maybe it was the other program that's on at the same time. . . . Or did I hear it on NPR?"

Edwards Books' database holds forty thousand titles containing the word *family*. I tell this fact to the customer. She asks, "Can you read them to me?"

The store is only 3,500 square feet. So there's a lot we don't have on hand. Including all forty thousand titles containing the word *family*. And including men's furnishings. A guy once walked up to the counter and asked if we sold belts. He was told no, we don't sell belts, and the fact that this is a bookstore was pointed out.

"OK, sorry," he said apologetically, before pausing and adding, "Would you have any suspenders?"

Whoever they are, whatever they want, they stand on

the other side of a forty-two-inch-high U-shaped counter, giving title and author, if they have that information, or unfolding newspaper reviews, or a loose-leaf note found on the kitchen table: "Daddy get me Judy Moody: *Judy Moody Was in a Mood. Not a Good Mood. A Bad Mood.*" Sometimes they possess the information down to the author's middle initial and the book's ISBN, which you can translate the way it strikes me, as "I Sell Books Now," or to the original meaning, International Standard Book Number, the ten-digit identification assigned to every published book in the world.

Most of the time, I'm given a lot less to go by.

"There is a dog on the cover, but it's not about a dog. It's got a chapter about a discovery that took place somewhere, but the whole story isn't about that. There was a copy over there last time I was here. It's not there now. Maybe somebody moved it? Or maybe it's sold? Do you know where it is?"

Knowing the exact location of the book with the dog on the cover and with the discovery on the pages inside was not a lifelong goal. Like every job I've ever held, bookselling just fell from the sky. So I add it to a formal employment history that began when I was a seven-year-old mucking out stalls in exchange for riding privileges on Star, a twenty-seven-year-old pinto pony, and continued in this order: 4-H cookie pusher (yes, we 4-H'ers had fundraising cookie campaigns, an idea the Girl Scouts probably stole from us); parish altar and statue duster (except for anything above the waist of the taller saints and God, as I was, and remain, frightened of heights); YMCA camp counselor (a career cut tragically short a mere two weeks into the summer by mononucleosis, though I was at camp long enough to get my official counselor polo shirt and pose—lined up very near those cute boys from Wilbraham—for the group photo); seller of Christmas trees and ill-shaped, half-dead wreaths (I did not raise the trees but admit to being responsible for the ill-shaped, half-dead stuff); hairnet-wearing grocery-store meat-department wrapper (a big factor in my eventual conversion to vegetarianism); photographer of other girls' boyfriends (commissioned by the other girls, I should clarify); high school hockey reporter writing about my high school's team (a team that went 0–30, yet, loving hockey, and maybe a few of the guys on the team, I never ran out of positive adjectives); server of pierogi and *golombki* and other ethnic specialties bought at the kitchen window of a polka pavilion, Pulaski Park, AKA The Polka Capital of New England, smack across the street from my childhood home in Three Rivers, Massachusetts; tampon purse-container packer (my village's other claim to fame, the Tampax factory, was eleven houses down the street, hired students during the summer, and gave the bonus of a free box every month); college-years charter-boat hook baiter (another nail in the coffin of my carnivorism); Howard Johnson's eight P.M. to two A.M. waitress (until the guy with the gun walked in the front door and I walked out the back); Papa Gino's hostess (yes, Papa Gino's has hostesses, and this franchise's boss was a guy named Bronce, a name I'd never heard of before or since); knitter of fancy sweaters sold to tourists (one sweater would take me a month to complete; I got paid thirty dollars per sweater—you do the math; apparently, I never did until writing this); postcollege newspaper reporter (my first full-time job—work I loved and did for most of fifteen years); ten months as co-owner of an ill-fated craft store (more often than the ring of the cash register was the sound of someone sneering to their co-browser, "Put that down! I can make you one of those for nothing!"); and author. In the last decade, I've had four novels and a memoir published. Published and distributed and sitting, as will be this book, on the shelves of bookstores worldwide. Bookstores including Bruce's. And Janet's.

I am now an author working in a bookstore. I am a spy from another land. Not unlike a dairy farmer hanging around the cheese shop. A fashion designer lurking in the boutique. A movie producer hunched down in the last row of the theater. The baker in the doorway when her candle-blazing cake is carried into the room. The quarterback hiding in the back seat during the fans' ride home. I know what it's like to create the work; now I am finding out what it's like to watch that work meet its audience. I don't mean just my own book—though I have sold those, an act that is a surreal completion of the full circle that began a few years earlier, when somewhere in dream or walk or conversation or scan of the classifieds I got the spark for what would become the book for which I'm now taking Visa or MasterCard and asking, "Can I wrap that for you," and "Do you need parking validation?" I'm talking about watching any author's book find a home. What I witness at Janet's is something every writer should be privy to for at least a day. Over and over again, the customers' reactions when just the right title is suggested or discovered or picked up after the arrival of a long-awaited special order. It's a range of emotions that, in the case of those purchasing books on some problem you'd rather not know existed, can be quiet gratitude, but more often because, more often, titles are related to leisure reading or pleasant, free-time activities, I would not be overstating to describe customers as delighted, joyful, and sometimes downright giddy when they approach the counter with their finds: the newest from their all-time favorite mystery writer, or a Complete Idiot's Guide to some pursuit about which they honestly do feel totally lacking in knowledge, or a book no bigger than a wallet that contains just the inspiration they need.

All writers work in some version of the storied garret. Some of us occupy that sort of cramped and angled space because of the constraints of finances. Others, despite having landed the advance check for the purchase of a chicly spartan downtown writing loft, remain in the attic simply as a romantic stab at tradition. For most of a decade, I wrote in a converted bedroom. But in the past few years since acquiring a portable laptop, I have spent winter days migrating from room to room as the low sun crawls along the southern half of the house, and summers typing away in a screened patio. For some writers, the solitude is simply a state of mind. Many of my literary brothers and sisters with more on their daily commitment plate fit their writing in where they can—in the bathroom because it's the only quiet place in the house, in the bleachers at Junior's coed anti-score-keeping T-ball game, in the office whenever the boss isn't looking. Monica Wood, whose *The Pocket Muse* is my newest, most favorite writing book, tells of finishing her first novel during a period of caring for a friend's baby. Despite her concerns about needing to be in a stone-quiet studio in order to create, Monica wrote her book on a notepad balanced on the handle of the stroller—even propped on the back of the napping infant. Monica finished her book with noisy life going on all around her. The solitude was in her head. And that solitude, whether on a houseboat on the Abitibi or in the skull, is the writer's common denominator. If we are lucky enough to get published, and extra lucky enough to be sent on a tour, or if we arrange a tour on our own dimes, then we poke our heads out for the duration of the promotion, afterward returning to our writing caves to begin something new. In between, the readings and signings give us an inkling of what a certain book can mean to a reader. I know they did that for me. Most amazing was when I would sign a copy for a reader who was effusing about how my book meant something extraordinary—and she or he was not even a relative. But to spend the day in a bookstore and witness that kind of gushing repeated hour after hour over a range of titles—from motocross to gluten-free diets to black holes to the Koran to whatever point in the alphabet Sue Grafton currently is up to—has spelled out for me in blinking and underlined neon the importance of information, of story, of creativity, of the written word. And I don't have to drag you over to the Travel section to point out how many places in this world would not permit the dissemination of half the topics we carry—if those countries permit bookstores at all.

According to the current edition of *American Book*

Trade Directory, here in the land of free speech we have our choice of 24,738 bookstores, including 11,410 branches of chains and 12,459 independents. Industry insiders will tell you that a truer measure of the number of full-line trade bookstores is more like 1,110, which is the number of stores that participate in the American Booksellers Association's Book Sense program aimed at raising awareness about what independent bookstores have to offer. Those in the know also tell you that the entire U.S. bookselling universe contains a mere three hundred or so truly outstanding stores.

Whatever their level of fascination or competence, bookstores in America are faced with the challenge of offering what they can hold of the 150,000 new titles published annually in what the directory calls "a swelling tide of new books" up almost 6 percent from the previous year. Fiction is the most robust category, hatching more than 17,000 new titles and editions, and books for juveniles are at their highest-ever number—more than 10,000. Edwards Books stocks 26,000 titles, a number that fluctuates with the seasons, the end-of-the-year holidays being the busiest, and the dog days of summer the slowest. Can't find what you want on the shelves? That's what special ordering's all about. The supplier has warehouses just bulging with all you could ever want to read, and it'll take only a day or two to get your book into your hands.

At No Extra Charge adds the sign behind the counter, where three wide shelves hold the special-order books awaiting pickup. Shelves that once held *Helping the Heart.*

OK, I can't recall if it was called *Helping the Heart* exactly, but the title was something close to that the first time I waited on a reader who'd gotten the phone call saying her special order had arrived.

I know the title was something about a heart. And about helping it. I don't know if it was medical or psychological assistance, but that doesn't matter here. What does is that this book was just what the woman needed. She told me her last name and I went over to the hold shelf and found this helping book and held it out to her to make sure it was the right one before I started to ring it up, and she took it in her hands and stared at the cover for a lot longer than you'd really need to read a three-word title. Then she clutched the book hard to her chest and smiled and said something about this being just the thing and she'd been waiting for, for so long—at least it seemed like long to her. I did see actual tears collecting and she was so sincere in her emotion and joy that I almost forgot to ask for the money.

The hugging to the chest is something I see often in the store. Maybe it's a natural way to hold a book, as there is sort of a natural way to hold an infant or a watermelon. But since taking note of it, I have observed that people in the CVS downstairs don't walk up and down those aisles with even the most costly Pantene clutched to their bosoms. And as much as they might have loved that meal they just had around the corner at Gus and Paul's, I never see them leaving there gently cradling their Styrofoam containers filled with leftover corned beef. Yet, at Edwards, these same CVS and Gus and Paul's customers hug books. As if between the covers is something precious, sacred, beloved. Different gods—CEOs, galactic raiders, left-handed pitchers, do-it-yourself divas, a boy wizard on his long-awaited new adventure—but each of them adored by somebody.

I watch the customers browse, select, hug, pay, hug again, leave, and return on another day in search of something else. I watch it all. I'm a spy, a fly on the shelf-lined wall. One who'll now add to those shelves the story of her first year of working in a bookstore.

WHEN I WAS A CHILD, MY TOWN HAD NO BOOK-
stores. I am well into adulthood at this point, and we still
don't have a traditional one. But you're all set if you want
the used, or the smutty. Several years ago, the volunteers
at my town's library rented a space in a former schoolhouse
and opened The Book Loft, last stop for all the books
donated to the library's annual book sale and first stop
for local bargain-hunting readers. And over on Main Street
there is an "adult" book-and-video enterprise adjacent to
the space once occupied by the fabric store where I used to
buy yards of paisley cotton to sew into my high school hal-
ter tops and peasant skirts. You certainly can buy books in
Palmer, Massachusetts. But if you're looking to purchase,
say, a brand-new travel guide to Dallas, rather than a 1998
edition, or a VHS of Debbie doing that particular munic-
ipality, you'll be out of luck.

Throughout my childhood, if I craved something new to read, I went to a library.

In my parochial grammar school, there was a makeshift library in the office, a small, dark, rectangular room where the worst kids got reprimanded and where inoculations were given and where confessions were heard by the pastor whenever the entire school was scheduled for a soul cleaning but a storm kept us from being able to march to the church next door. Most of the books in the school library were, of course, religious. Selfless saints tackling all manner of beasts and infidels and temptations. Nothing against saints and all, but I was more interested in something I could relate to. I liked to read about girls because, well, I was one. I liked to read about outdoorsy girls because that's the type I was. I liked adventure stories because, though I didn't often experience adventures, I regularly dreamed them up. I ran with like-minded girlfriends through the woods, the fields, along the river, playing at being orphans escaped from the orphanage, or imagining ourselves explorers just approaching the fringes of some undiscovered society. Through the rhododendron bushes at the edge of the LaBontes' backyard, we'd observe their hanging the laundry or mowing the lawn as activities of an alien culture. Many other days, I'd strike out alone and pretend I was Donn Fendler.

I found Donn in fifth grade, and he was a big surprise, most of the other kids in the books on his shelf being holy ones who in some century ages back refused to turn from their beliefs and got horribly martyred. The only bad thing that ever happened to young Donn Fendler was getting lost for a week or so in the Maine woods. I preferred his story because I'd been on camping vacations in Maine, and I practically lived in the woods behind my house. Again and again, as a child will repeat a favorite story, I read *Lost On a Mountain In Maine,* which was subtitled "A true saga of courage and hope in the wilderness of Maine's Mount Katahdin." Back in 1939, Donn was a twelve-year-old Boy Scout who took a wrong turn off Mount Katahdin's summit and away from his hiking party, and for the nine days until he stumbled, starving and half-naked, into the backyard of a remote fishing camp luckily occupied that day by fishermen, he fended off mosquitoes and even the occasional bear with no complaint stronger than his curious trademark exclamation of "Christmas!" By day, I read Donn; by afternoon, following supper and homework, I became him, wandering the measly couple of acres of wood behind my father's vegetable garden, making invisible the backs of the houses and silencing the polka recordings playing from the speakers in the Frydryks' backyard, and pretending I was in the middle of nowhere, desperately searching for a way home. Just before dark, I'd stagger dazed and confused onto neatly trimmed lawn, past swing set and inverted rubber-tire planter, my journey home over for that day.

Stories fueled me in that manner. I'd repeat them in my head, act out my versions, invent ongoing sagas in which I became a character. Intellectual Nancy Drew didn't have enough of the kind of fun I liked. I preferred her tomboyish contemporary, Trixie Belden, who, in the first book of her series of girlish horseish adventures, faced the fangs of a poisonous copperhead. Whenever asked by my mother to go down to the corner to buy a half pound of thin-sliced Polish ham and a loaf of Dreikorn's, which was often, I morphed into Trixie. I rolled from beneath the stairs the royal blue Columbia on which I'd learned to ride, but in actuality I was leading my prizewinning quarter horse from her stall. I pedaled down the street, but it really was a horse carrying me, and the wind elevating my braids was from her cinematic gallop, not my string-bean, scabby-kneed legs pumping away. And when I leaned the bike against the wall of Lis's store, I'd just dropped her reins. No need to tie her because the horse and I had the kind of bond that would have her standing there even if a carrot festival was ten feet away.

That same horse carried me to my other source for books. My town's library was a five-mile ride, but I rarely needed to make the trip. The Palmer Public Library came to me, in the form of a hulking, pale green truck known as the bookmobile. Once a week, as part of its regular route through the four villages that comprise Palmer, it would roll to a stop in front of my grammar school. In the summer months, I visited the bookmobile at its stop at the public elementary school down the hill from my home. Over the years, the Columbia might have been made mod with the begged-for conversion kit of metallic blue banana seat and rabbit-ear handlebars, but it retained the nerdish woven-wire basket into which I piled all the books I was allowed to check out in a single visit. Mrs. Bigda, the librarian, and her cohort and driver, Mrs. Rehor, knew to direct me to the newest animal stories—especially those about horses and dogs—the selection of how-tos (draw, paint, knit, or do just about any other type of arty or crafty thing), the picture books of other lands, especially those in which people rode horses and played with dogs and painted and knit or did just about any other such activity. The two ladies never confined me to the bookmobile's bottommost rows, where the titles for the youngest readers were found. I read ahead for my age, and, in fourth grade, after hearing Sister Mary Jane mention a guy named Albert Schweitzer, I picked out and polished off his 1953 *Out of My Life and Thought*. I don't remember if they gave extra credit for phone-directory-thick autobiographies of your more famous humanitarians, but I recall being adamant about filling each of the lines on the library's summer reading club bookmark, the honor system through which members earned prizes I've long forgotten. What is memorable: the smooth, marbled feel to the red or blue paper bookmarks, and the U-shaped slit to fit over the top of a page. Every summer I asked for more than one, because every summer I'd read more than the dozen or so that could be listed on a single bookmark. Not because I was a literary kiss-ass. I simply liked to read.

I can thank my grandmother for that. I was raised one floor above my maternal grandparents, and our daily contact resulted in a host of blessings, among them a head start on reading. While other kids my age trundled off to preschool or kindergarten, I attended my own private academy thirteen steps down the back porch. One day when I was five, Babci plunked in front of me a hardbound copy of *The Cat in the Hat,* and with that book taught me how to read. Dr. Seuss had been born and raised twenty or so miles away, in the city of Springfield, so the choice of author was a natural. The poppy prose and wild drawings made the learning fun, though I distinctly recall how nervous the story made me as the cat took all manner of liberties in a home that wasn't even his to wreck. Even so, I quickly and fearlessly graduated to the sequel, *The Cat in the Hat Comes Back,* then went on to Seussian tales less anxiety provoking—*Hop on Pop, Go Dog Go, One Fish Two Fish Red Fish Blue Fish*—and I never looked back. Babci had made me privy to the most amazing of codes, and I caught on so well that when I entered first grade it was insulting to be handed the fabric-paged, facile *Tip and Mitten,* the three-words-per-page dog-and-cat story through which my fellow first graders were to learn to read. I breezed through its dozen pages while most of my classmates were still sobbing with first-day separation anxiety, and within days Sister Tobia had me spending recess tutoring a clueless first grader who these days would probably be labeled learning disabled and given all sorts of professional help, but in our tiny six-room eight-grade parish school, the extra assistance he needed came from me, still five years of age.

Four years later, around the same time I found Donn Fendler, a neat twist happened in my own life story. Mrs. Bigda of bookmobile fame was pals with my mother, and, with her, co-led the aforementioned cookie-selling Crafty Critters 4-H Club that met each Friday in the Bigdas' finished basement. Mrs. Bigda mentioned needing an extra driver for the bookmobile and asked my mother if she'd be interested. After a few driving lessons and the DMV test for a truck license, the job was hers. My home life so far had been rather Beaver Cleaver–like. Maybe my mother didn't wear shirtdresses and pearls while preparing dinner, but, like Mrs. Cleaver, she always had been home when I left for school, and had been there waiting when I returned. So I simultaneously began to experience the sad echo of an empty house at the end of my school day and the braggy thrill that I had a mother strong and cool enough to pilot an enormous truck of books wherever she wanted to. Look! It's my very own mother driving all those stories to Saints Peter and Paul and over to the French school and out to Lake Thompson! Once a week, the following summer, when I biked down to return my books and select new ones, my trip didn't stop there. When the books moved on, I did too. Despite whining, I wasn't allowed onboard while the bookmobile was moving, so I pedaled to the next stop, and hopped aboard in time to help release the big, long elastic cords that were secured across the shelves to keep the collection in place while in transit. My mother and Mrs. Bigda let me help here and there, neatening shelves, handing out bookmarks, even checking out books, a process that included stamping the return date on the pocket pasted inside each book, and stamping the same date on a card kept on file until the book was returned. I loved the stamping. I loved the filing. I loved all the bits of paper and the lines and boxes that needed to be checked, and I believe that was the start of a lifelong office-product fixation that causes me to slam on the brakes at the sight of a Staples.

The books I owned I kept close, in a long and low blond-varnished shelving unit in the room my sister and I shared at the end of the hall. The top shelf held an array of dolls (hers) and horse statues (mine). The middle shelf bore games and art supplies. The bottom one was packed with books (shared). There was a shoelace-bound scrap-book fat with copies of *Highlights* magazine, to which my sister had once been given a subscription. There was a heavy concentration of books telling animal stories, and I remember a lot on rabbits. *Home for a Bunny* was a real estate odyssey in which a young rabbit checked out the op-tions of living beneath rocks and logs and other country-side vacancies. In *Peter Rabbit,* a sneak into the produce aisle of Mr. MacGregor's garden results in getting chased by a hoe-wielding farmer. The *Aesop's Fables* collection in-cluded a line drawing illustrating in detail the moral of each story—more rabbits, to be sure, but also wolves and snakes and the odd weasel. My sister and I had a stack of those thin cardboard Golden Books with their trademark golden-papered spines, many of them containing animals too, many of them big-eyed and nattily attired, most of them experiencing further states of distress. Hunger, evic-tions, runs for their lives, Donn Fendlers in feathers and short pants, each searching for home. Just as I'd worried about the consequences eventually awaiting the kids whose home was being trashed by the *Cat in the Hat,* I sweated about the fates of the animal characters. Even if I'd read the same story a million times, halfway through I'd still get that sick turning of the stomach. You could tell me, "It's only a story," but I knew that what was in my hands was more than ink on paper.

Thankfully, the shelf in my room also contained some angst-free nonfiction. Because I could be a ham, I once re-ceived a present of a bright green hardcover titled some-thing like *100 Jokes and Riddles.* None of them were very funny if you weren't seven or eight or drunk, but that didn't stop me from Henny Youngmanning it up at family gatherings. There also was a picture book of Poland, land of my grandparents, and, if you were judging from the rose gardens and castles and thatched-roof villages in which everyone wore elaborately embroidered clothing, land where nothing bad ever happened, and you'd never in a million years give even one thought to moving your life halfway across the world. Because I loved hockey, I loved my copy of *Orr on Ice*, megastar-Boston-Bruins-defenseman Bobby Orr's photo-filled biography that began with a series of full-page pictures of him dressing for a game, starting with long underwear and athletic cup. At that point, I loved horses more than boys, so somebody had given me a copy of *The Equine Bible.* Nothing more upsetting in there than a quick description of bloat. We had a regular Bible, too, a children's version with a color-photo insert showing an altar boy's duties as he assisted a pre–Vatican II priest who said Mass with his back to the parishioners and, when he turned, was seen to be reading his own Bible with the aid of thick Clark Kent–style glasses.

Most of these books had been bought half an hour west, at Johnson's Bookstore in Springfield, a very popular and proper Main Street mainstay that slipped your purchases into hunter-green paper bags on which a stylized sailboat glided. A few blocks away, at the base of The Victoria Hotel, which would be leveled in the mid-'60s to make way for the city's first civic center, my grandparents operated a restaurant that we in the family called The Restaurant but that everybody else called The Square Lunch. So my sister and I were brought into the city often, trips that provided me with my first opportunities to see buildings that were taller than two stories, people whose skin color was different than mine, and a genuine full-service bookstore.

I remember best the air. Johnson's smelled of possibility. Something emitted by the pages in all those books on all those shelves. Here is where you can learn this, meet them, get lost, maybe find your way. This first bookstore of my world was high-ceilinged like a church, and as quiet as one. Many shoppers, but little noise, as each of them was absorbed in something on the cover or the page before them. The only sounds: soft questions asked of clerks, and the bell on the pre-electronics register ringing like pinged crystal. The front of the store was nothing but books. Wooden shelves lined the room, tables took up the center, then rows of shelves as you progressed toward the rear. The back third or so was stationery. Racks of fine boxed paper and greeting cards all awaiting your signature and any words you cared to add. Downstairs was early Staples: shelves of virgin notebooks and reams of typing paper, cardboard boxes of unsharpened Ticonderogas, glass cases holding expensive pens. The same floor included toys. Nothing chintzy—quality wooden building sets and kits for schooners and biplanes that were advertised by the finished products done up perfectly there in front of you. One set of stairs up from the main floor were gifts and office accessories like you see in movies: globes bearing ancient sea-dragon-crawling maps, weighty metal bookends shaped like actual books, serious-looking blotters with triangles of embossed leather at each corner. Complicated barometers and mantel clocks and brass letter openers. Go down to the main floor again, out the back door, cross the courtyard and walk into a second building, with a first floor devoted entirely to art supplies. More of the smell of paper, here grand, wide sheets of it with the ragged edges that told you it was handmade. Tubes of paint stocked in drawers organized by subtleties of color. Brushes I put to my skin. Delicate easels, an entire wall of wood from which they would build you a frame. Last stop, upstairs: a labyrinth of used books. Magazines, too. I know the layout so well because I patronized Johnson's from those childhood days up to its closing, when a spiraling economy and a downtown "in transition" forced it to fold in 1998 at one hundred and fifteen years of age. To pay homage, walk down Main Street and look for City Sportswear, a clothing store of all things athletic.

As a teen, I would pick up CliffsNotes at the Waldenbooks half an hour from my home in the Eastfield Mall, a now thirty-six-year-old creation of shopping-mall pioneer The Rouse Company. In Eastfield's first heyday, when I bought Levi's corduroys at The Lodge and queued for *No Nukes* in one of its two-count-'em-two theaters, Waldenbooks became my closest new-books source. The mall recently experienced a renovation that brought to our neck of the woods the vital Old Navy and a complex of no less than sixteen movie theaters. The Waldenbooks remains, though newcomer Pam's Paperbacks, five minutes east, is now the bookstore closest to home.

In the year of my country's Bicentennial, I made my own history by graduating from high school and heading off to Portland, Maine, to study photography at an art school then called the Portland School of Art, now called the Maine College of Art. Located in a struggling little city that could claim but a single trendy little street—Exchange—carved from a seedy waterfront area, now it's thick in a forest of gentrification regularly selected by *Newsweek* and *Utne* as one of the country's coolest cities. I'm not sure of the number of bookstores Portland has now, but back then I knew only one. There's still a store—Books Etc.—in that storefront just up the hill from where I once baited those hooks.

I spent the first four years after college working as a reporter back in Springfield, at what was then called the *Daily News.* On Thursday afternoons, after Laurie Vanasse handed out the paychecks from her top lefthand drawer, I would make a beeline for the corner of Main and Hampden, where I'd deposit a decent sum into my savings account at Third National Bank, and take the rest in cash, much too much of which was spent next-door at Johnson's Bookstore, conveniently connected to Third National by an inner door. That entrance should have been shaped like a funnel, because that's what it was for me. Money from the one building being poured right into the next. I was beginning to travel, and bought some of my first guides there, the Let's Go! I used to explore the coast of California, the maps of New England woods, the little Berlitz book of basic French that would help me out in both the old and new cities of Montreal. My job had landed me in a desk across from columnist and avid knitter Zedra Aranow, who refueled in me interest in the skill I'd used to make those thirty-dollar sweaters back in art school. I still have the book on Latvian mittens that I found at Johnson's, each page the key to more dizzyingly colored patterns, and, should you be a stickler for authenticity, each page translated into Latvian. There I also bought Stephen King's *The Shining,* the first book that kept me up all night, reading, then trembling.

Several of my Johnson purchases were write-offs. The maps in *Let's Go: New York City* helped me to navigate Manhattan in the early '80s, when the paper sent me to cover the spring and fall fashion previews that then were held for two weeks each April and October. As a feature writer, I often interviewed authors, and if copies of my subjects' books didn't show up in the mail as the publicists had promised, I'd run to Johnson's. In a conference room at the University of Hartford, I clutched a copy of *Roots* as I sat at a huge conference table edged with reporters interviewing Alex Haley. This was several years after the phenomenal success of his 1976 classic, and Haley was an enormous star. In person he proved courteous, and he turned the tables, interviewing the reporters because he'd once worked as one and wanted to know what the newspaper business was like for us youngsters. At the Springfield Marriott, I brought my Johnson's-bought copy of *Sybil* along when I interviewed Flora Rheta Schrieber, biographer of child abuse survivor Sybil Isabel Dorsett. Flora Rheta had introduced Sybil to the psychoanalyst who helped to discover her sixteen separate and distinct personalities, all of whom were brought to life in a 1976 Emmy Award–winning television performance by

Sally Field. When I knocked, Flora Rheta was at the window, painting the Connecticut River as it flowed south below her hotel, and she continued her painting the entire time we spoke.

My purchases at Johnson's changed as did my life and circle. In what would turn out to be a waste of time and postage, I spent many Thursday afternoons at the back of the first floor, selecting embarrassingly tacky and romantic greeting cards meant as CPR for a fizzling long-distance relationship. Friends began to marry, so I visited the gift section for slate cheese tray after slate cheese tray wrapped in my choice of the fancy paper kept on fat rolls behind the counter. Friends began procreating, so at Johnson's I bought the first of what has been my standard baby gift for the twenty-two years since: Jim Trelease's now-longtime international megamillion best seller, *The Read Aloud Handbook*. My best friend was killed, and I discovered the self-help aisle as I sought Rabbi Harold Kushner's *When Bad Things Happen to Good People,* the classic that had just then been published and that everyone was telling me to read. Soon, full of the realization that I could be gone in an instant too, I purchased my dream home ("Do you have anything on home repair?"), a sweet A-frame on the shores of a little lake on which I launched a secondhand Gloucester Gull Dory ("Do you have anything on sailing?"). Newly engaged, I visited Johnson's to scoop up a wedding planner. Newly married, I picked up cellophane-page albums in which to organize the photographic evidence. My last purchase of those years: a 1984 map of southern New England, to be consulted as I began a new job at the *Providence Journal.*

* * *

I continued to live in Western Massachusetts, and, when not driving my car into the ground during the two years I worked in Providence, I patronized those same bookstores near my home. But for the past ten years, my bookstore experience has greatly expanded. With the release of each of my previous five books, I've been sent on promotional tours, most of them spans of three weeks spent largely traveling from bookstore to bookstore, meeting and greeting and reading and signing and answering questions like, "How much money do you make" and "Did you know my little boy here is an author, too?" Book tours are arranged by your publicist, who contacts stores and sets up events to maximize the time you have in a town or city. Readings and signings often are scheduled night after night, and when you add interviews and radio or television appearances, there might be half-a-dozen obligations in a single day. Drop-in signings can fill gaps in the schedule, or, as happened to me during my last visit to Chicago, comprise your entire day. Drop-ins sound just like what they are: you stop in a bookstore and ask for the manager and the manager comes out and with an "OK, what are you selling?" look on his or her face and you say some form of "Hi, I'm an author on a book tour. Would you have my book in stock, and, if so, can I sign the copies? If not, would you please order some for your store?" Sometimes they have your new book. Sometimes the store has your new book as well as some or all of your backlist, and copies are located and you sign them while the manager affixes on each cover little emblems that read Signed by the Author and the books are then placed near the register so customers can see they are signed and, because many people like the idea of autographed copies, maybe get interested in buying one. Sometimes the store will not have your book in stock and the manager will take the information and promise to order it. Sometimes the manager will do this right in front of you, inviting you around to the other side of the counter and showing you the computer screen and typing in a number that will enable the book to be ordered from the store's distributor. Sometimes the manager will do all that and also offer to give you a tour of the store, will point out the framed black-and-whites of famous literati who've read there, will show you their favorite titles in the recommended section and tell you that your book definitely will be read and just might end up there. Then, if there is a café on-site, you might get treated to a beverage and a baked good. There are the rare drop-ins during which you wish a roadrunner-like anvil would drop onto the head of the bored bookstore employee who responds with a bland, "And?" after you enthusiastically explain yourself and your book and the reason you woke at four A.M. to fly to this city halfway across the country. Whatever the reception, you hop in the car and go off to the next store to do all of the above again.

The car belongs to the local literary escort. If you were not in need of a literary escort, you probably would not be aware that such people exist. But they're out there, I've learned, ferrying literary types sunrise to moonrise, from event to TV studio to hotel to airport. Your publisher sees no sense in trusting that, in a town you've never seen before and probably never heard of prior to your arrival this morning at 7:23, you'll be able to get yourself to the locations of the local *Good Morning* [insert town] radio program and the *NewsCenter* [insert channel] noontime broadcast or to the city room of the [insert city] *Gazette* and the afternoon of drop-in signings and then to the evening's bookstore. So your publisher hires one of the many literary escorts who assist those who are running around promoting. In each large city—even some of the smaller ones—you'll stumble off the plane to find a bright-eyed, smiling literary escort holding, instead of your name magic-markered on a card, a copy of your book. That aforementioned all-drop-in-signing-day in Chicago, my escort was Bill Young, a lively, chatty guy whose business card read

BILL YOUNG
(Not a Ph.D.)

He might not have a doctorate, but Bill has the ubiquitous enormous literary-escort car and the ubiquitous enormous literary-escort knowledge of his turf, in this case Chicagoland, as people in and around Chicago call their area, and on that one day, between when he picked me up at the Oprah-touted all-suite Omni hotel at nine A.M. and delivered me back there at eleven P.M., we dropped in at twenty-two stores from one end of Chicagoland to the other. A day like that can be exhausting and probably can addle even those authors who've written books on serenity. Some days on a book tour you're so busy you don't remember your title, never mind the city you're in, and you very soon come to hate the sound of your own voice, especially as it describes over and over your plot, and your particular path to publication—the answers to two of the most frequently asked questions. But unless there's a revival of the accordion, a book tour is the closest I'm ever going to come to knowing an iota of the musician's legendary life on the road. And I never want to complain, simply because of the sheer fact that I get to do this. Traveling, and meeting the readers who, in essence, are the people who keep me in business. You're sent to states where you have no relatives for a thousand miles—yet there is a room full or half full or a quarter full of people waiting to read your words. Or maybe, as was the case for me one night, there are only two people, and one of the two has sat down only in order to finish her latte. But still, somebody has shown up, somebody is interested, somebody wants to read what you've written. When you consider the innumerable numbers who would give their writing hands to get published, and when you consider that you've actually been published—and now a stretch limo has been hired to take you the block from your hotel to the studios of *Today*—well, any of the above are nice problems to have.

I've been on book tours that have taken me from coast to coast, and in one stretch of twelve months I made no fewer than two hundred appearances at bookstores, book fairs, and libraries, as well as at church picnics and hospital gift shops. Inside, outside, in all weather. When I was promoting my third novel, my reading at the Odyssey Bookshop in South Hadley coincided with a hurricane warning. I phoned store owner Joan Grenier, whose late father, Romeo, began the business in his drugstore in 1964.

"Let me know when you want to reschedule," I told her, as the trees in my yard began to dance the YMCA.

"But people have been calling," Joan told me. "They say they'll come if you will."

I had nothing else planned but a night hiding out in my basement with a transistor radio and a bag of Doritos, so I hopped in my car. The way I saw it, and as this very sentence proves, a reading in a hurricane would make a story somewhere down the line. Plus, the Odyssey had been good to me from my literary start. So there I was, reading before the maybe dozen rubber-coated readers, the rain lashing at the window, another adventure in promotion. Mine is not a household name, so, the way I see it, I need to do whatever I can to get the word out about my books. Therefore, in the past ten years, many times over, I have been an author visiting a bookstore. But I am now an author working in a bookstore, thick in the entire experience. From opening to closing, from ordering to receiving, stocking the shelves with the new books, removing the ones that are past their prime, setting up displays, taking them down when their reason for being has passed, trying to find an answer to the question of "what would you recommend...." and when I press into a reader's hands my answer—say, William Least Heat-Moon's cross-country epic *Blue Highways* or *Rattlebone*, Maxine Clair's cross-the-Kansas-City-tracks collection of linked short stories—I tell the person, "If you don't like it, you can bring it back, but I promise you, you're going to love it." Right then I am doing for William Least Heat-

Moon or for Maxine and their books what I witnessed Janet Edwards doing for me and for my fledgling career on an afternoon I visited her store shortly after my first novel was published. I can still see her standing at the right-hand side of the counter, handing an Ohio salesman my book with the guarantees, "If you don't like it, you can bring it back, but I promise you, you're going to love it." There was no way she could have known I would be walking through the door at that very moment. Her enthusiasm for my book was not for show. It was just what Janet does well, and genuinely, for books written by many authors she'll never meet—much less ask to fill out a W-2 form—and it is what I've come to learn is called hand selling, and it is what I would come to do myself, at that very counter, and very unexpectedly.

In March 2001, I was traveling on my own little space odyssey. My new millennium had begun with an unnerving doctor's appointment, and in a dizzying nine months I went from a battery of tests to a diagnosis of breast cancer to surgery to treatment, and had begun 2001 with a big case of the confusing "what now?" period all the many cancer books I'd read had correctly warned me would hit. For many months you go through being cared for and checked on nearly every day and then you're spat out into the world to resume your life. Now what? you wonder. What's going to get me now? Or what should I be doing now so something won't get me? Or how should I be living now that I still have a chance to live? In late winter of 2001, I was heavy into the weighing of all the above questions, and on one particular March Saturday afternoon, was squished up in an armchair doing more weighing when Janet phoned the house to say that she was looking for some help at the bookstore. An older Ruth who'd retired had been replaced indefinitely by a younger Ruth, who'd just decided to return to school. Help would be needed for only a few hours a week—please spread the word.

I scanned my mind's Rolodex for people who either were in need of a job or who would like to work in a bookstore or who just needed to get out of the house and do something different. When I got to the S's, I saw my own name. After yet another session of weighing, I dialed Janet and asked, "Do you have an employee discount?"

"Sure, why? Do you know of somebody for the job?"

"Yeah. Me."

Janet laughed her genuine ha-ha-ha. Assured me, "You don't want to work here."

"Why not?"

She gave me the answer you'd want a bookseller to give, that I should be working on a new book—she knew I owed my publisher a novel—"You need to write."

I told her, "I need to get out of here."

Back in whatever normal was for me, I loved being alone. But lately, the what-nows were making alone time a little too creepy. I was well aware that I needed to write, but I also was feeling I needed to be away from my office at home and in an environment that had no connection to the past year. I rambled some version of that to Janet, and I'm not sure she got it all, but some bits must have emerged clearly enough because there she was telling me that she wanted to help, and if coming to the store was what I needed, I would be more than welcome. I told her I was worried about a couple of things: I was still blown out from radiation treatments, and still napped each day around three, so if she needed me in the afternoon, I might need to lie down at some point. Also, I added, does it matter that I'm pretty much unable to count?

"We have a calculator, and we have a pile of cardboard in the back room, you can lie down whenever you need to," said Janet, who invited me to start the following Tuesday.

I hung up and walked upstairs to my calendar, which displayed thirty-one vacant boxes. I wrote *bookstore* crookedly in the Tuesday space, and, wondering what I'd consented to, went back to my chair.

"She's here!"

Janet can be loud.

Especially when you'd prefer she not be.

I'd just walked through the door. It was a little after noon, and noon, I would come to learn, is Edwards' busiest time of the day. The store caters to and relies upon the downtown business community, and many people spend their lunch hours at the store, browsing, picking up newspapers, checking out the new titles. That day, a line of people waited at the counter, and Janet, behind the counter, was crowing my arrival. After spending much of the past year out of the loop of life, I had gotten too close to agoraphobia. That first day, I didn't want my presence pointed out to anyone. It was my idea simply to slide into the bookstore, start alphabetizing the shelves, or whatever it is that people in bookstores do all day, and then I'd go home. My goal of getting out would have been reached, Janet would have had the extra help she'd sought, everybody would be happy. But it seemed that Janet was pleased far ahead of time.

"Look, she's here!"

A few of those in line turned around, weren't sure whom they were supposed to be checking out. Turned back to make their purchases.

From my signings at the store, I knew the location of the back room, home to those stacks of cardboard, and the essential passageway to the employee restroom. I went straight to the back room and closed the door. I knew that coats were hung behind that door, so that was one reason. But I also was wondering if there were a rear exit.

The door with its layer of coats pushed into me.

Janet.

"Here's the new help!"

She hugged me energetically. Took my hand. Led me back into the store. Stood me next to her behind the counter, to join her mother, Flo, and morning manager Pat. Flo and Pat wove without collision to and from the one cash register, and back again to assist the next customer. Janet answered the phone, tapped an author's name into the computer, and gave the caller the news that we not only carried the book in question but had two in stock and could she put one aside? I stood useless at her left, trying to stay out of the way. Shoppers approached, the phone rang again. I accepted a proffered fifty cents for a *Boston Globe,* put the stack of books Pat was ringing up into one of the white plastic bags imprinted with the red words THANK YOU THANK YOU THANK YOU. Somebody asked me for a dictionary. "Let me show you where those are," Janet said, to both the customer and me. At a set of shelves in the rear of the store, between Philosophy/Reference/ Drama and Children's, Janet and the customer and I stood in a circle as the variety of basic dictionaries were pointed out. Pocket-size, desk-size, gift set that is shrink-wrapped and includes a thesaurus. Janet gave the prices as I glanced at the top row, and its dictionaries of legal terms, rhyme, slang, and frequently misspelled words. The customer quizzed Janet on the merits of desk versus pocket; were there the same number of words in each? Ultimately, she decided upon the $5.99 copy, and when Janet said she'd ring it up, the woman responded, "Oh, not today."

We returned to the counter to find a woman mining her purse for the price of *A Child is Born,* a photography book on babies in utero, snapped by the tiniest of cameras as the subjects slept and divided cells and grew finger-prints and all your necessary organs and otherwise pre-pared themselves for their big one-way trip into the world. "This is a classic," Janet said, and she handed the book to me already flipped over so I'd see the ISBN that she told me to key into the register. I carefully entered the ten digits and then, as instructed, hit "scan" and "subto-tal" and had a sum to tell the customer, tax included. A baby book sold by a baby clerk. Change made with the help of the register that calculates all that for you, book placed in the bag complete with Edwards' bookmark, a query made as to whether parking validation was needed, thanks expressed—and I had accomplished my first transaction.

"Brian! Look who we have working here now!"

Janet again, loud again, to a mutual friend this time. Brian Trelease, investment firm exec and brother of *Read-Aloud* author Jim. Brian, whom I'd seen walking through the door, which is when I'd crouched out of sight. "Where's the dictionary?" I could handle. Possible questions about how I was feeling I felt unable to deal with. So I actually crawled into the cabinet at Janet's feet. I heard the snap of newspaper quarters being placed on the counter, and Brian's voice, and then Janet saying "I don't know where she went—Suzanne's working here now! She was here a minute ago. . . ."

When I heard her bid him a farewell, I waited a few seconds before pulling at her pant leg and asking in a pathetic voice, "Janet, could you not do that?"

She looked down, surprised by both me and the question. "What?"

"Don't tell people that I'm here. Please don't make a big deal of it."

Janet has these big eyes. She shot them down at me. She didn't understand. Or maybe she did. She said, "But you are here." And she had a point.

I was there. On earth. And now, in a bookstore. I stayed by her ankle as, above me, in the big old world, she dealt with a customer. Above me, in that same world, the phone

rang. I turned around for a sign of Flo and Pat. Saw nobody else. I reached my hand up from my place on the floor.
"Edwards Books," I said. And even though I felt a little
ill, and very ill equipped to make the offer, I added, "May
I help you?"

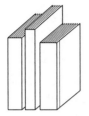

"MOTHER! MOTHER!"

Though I am nobody's mother, I look up from trying to learn the computer. The speaker is far from babyhood—as he is from childhood, teenhood and middle age. He's got to be in his seventies, and he's calling "Mother" in the direction of Flo, herself seventy-seven.

To clarify for me, the man points at Flo, who stands at her computer with back turned. The man has an accomplice, a shorter guy who's younger by maybe a decade. Both are in long dressy raincoats. The tall man holds a neatly folded plastic shopping bag.

Loudly this time, he calls: "Mother!"

Launched from her engrossment with the screen, Flo turns: "What? What?" Then a faux-disappointed, "Oh, it's you."

"'Hello, Mother!" The man is waving a Styrofoam box

of the type that is the last resting place for leftovers. "Brought you something!"

"Here comes trouble." That's Janet now. She's back from "down the hall," one of the first bits of bookstore parlance I learn. It's code for bathroom, the place from which Janet has emerged brushed and lipsticked and fresh for the afternoon's challenges. Forty-nine years of age, slim and dressed daily in all black Ann Taylor, Janet could be a poster child for women afraid that letting their hair go gray will make them look like hags. She wears hers shoulder-length, flipped up with the help of electric rollers. There are bangs that fall nearly to the cool black rectangular frames of her eyeglasses. Simple silver earrings. A silver necklace and matching bracelet that both lace through their individual hollow hearts. Janet reaches beneath the counter to a metal rack holding the newpapers that several regular customers prefer to have reserved. She hands the taller man a *New York Times* and a *Wall Street Journal*. He unfolds his plastic bag and slides the papers inside, then pays the two dollars. Janet cordially thanks the men, then introduces me to the shorter man, semiretired businessman Donald Keavany, and the taller man, totally retired John Breck, whose surname on all those bottles of shampoo is no coincidence: that's his family. Thus, I meet my first bookstore celebrity. The hair to an empire. But, really, just another guy picking up a paper, with a sense of humor and with the good sense to recycle a bag.

Donald and John spar with Janet and Flo, telling them it's about time there was some new blood in this place, maybe the service will improve. Lunchtime customers queuing don't end the routine; the men simply move aside and continue. "Brought you some cake," Donald says to Flo as he sets the box on the counter. "Baked it myself."

Flo lifts the lid to examine the offering as Donald asks, "What's this about?" pointing to the counter, where Eric Schlosser's newly released *Fast Food Nation: The Dark Side of the All-American Meal* is propped on a little wire stand. "It's about our lunch," John tells him. There are a few more cracks, then a couple of "Good day, ladies" and a march out the door.

Janet tells me that the pair meets for lunch downtown most days, sometimes with friends, but usually it's just the two of them. Lunch, and a stop at the bookstore to pick up papers, to leave what's normally half a ham salad sandwich, to get a few parking stickers, and a few laughs.

"Looks good! I'll have this after my cottage cheese," Flo says upon further inspection of the cake, and brings the box back to her computer.

The counter is in a squared-off U shape of maroon Formica with dark wood trim. A fat support column in its center has been sheathed in slotted wallboard onto which movable Plexiglas shelves can be attached. Three sides are display space. The front bears the three wide pressboard shelves on which the special order books are placed. Overflow is in a cardboard box below.

The U shape itself is a jumble of necessities. The front, ten feet in length, holds a computer that is actually a cash register. To the right of that is a PC. Add a little work space to the left of the first machine and to the right of the second, and that's all there's room for. On the nine-foot-long leg of the counter nearest the door, there's a clearing for dealing with customers, then a computer on which the ordering and inventory checking is done, and then there are maybe a few more feet of space. On the other nine-foot leg, there's a printer; a credit card machine; and Flo's computer, which is mainly used for inputting orders, and, at the end of each day, for making a record of the inventory. A couple more feet of space after that, usually filled with greeting cards to be returned and stacks of books to be returned, and that's it. Running along the edge of the counter, maybe ten inches from the surface, is a shelf on which items are displayed. There's a rack of postcards, a dollar for three, images of the Basketball Hall of Fame down the street and Smith College up in Northampton and the Bridge of Flowers way up in Shelburne Falls. Along the rest of the surface, more wire easels hold the current best sellers, or titles that have been getting a lot of attention, or simply books that the staff members are keen on. During my treatments the fall before, Janet had sent me Tracy Chevalier's *Girl with a Pearl Earring,* which was displayed on the counter next to Susan Vreeland's *Girl in Hyacinth Blue.* She pairs them because she loves the stories and for their odd link of being recent novels centering on Vermeer. Also propped up on this day are other new and notables: *The Bonesetter's Daughter,* by Amy Tan; Dave Eggers's debut autobiography, *A Heartbreaking Work of Staggering Genius;* Stephen King's *The Dreamcatcher;* and a stack of the latest Oprah book club pick, Gwyn Hyman Rubio's *Icy Sparks.*

I study the shelf because displays are one of the things Janet wants me to work on. Starting with the next biggie, St. Patrick's Day. Normally, titles for this holiday would have been in stock and stacked on a table near the door for a month already. There is an enormous Irish population in western Massachusetts. One of the store's constant best sellers, British journalist Cole Moreton's *Hungry for Home: Leaving the Blaskets: A Journey from the Edge of Ireland,* tells of one of the sources of that community—the abandoned Blasket Islands off the Dingle Peninsula on Ireland's southwestern coast—and follows them right here to Springfield, the city to which many of the islanders immigrated. So a St. Patrick's Day display will hold interest here. But, short on staff, Janet has had no time for building pyramids of *Angela's Ashes* way before customers even consider it might be time to start thinking green.

Like most people, I've gone into stores in August and felt irked as I tripped over pumpkins and ghosts and other Halloweenalia. But I've come to learn that's the way it works in retail. The very minute one special day or season is over, you lunge toward the next. Father's Day merchandise should be in place the day after Mother's Day, or you face the risk of income lost. On the same day that Christmas books are being marked 50 percent off, titles like *Bedroom Games* and *The Multi-Orgasmic Couple* are stacked up in anticipation of Valentine's Day. There are enough people who begin asking for next year's calendars at the end of the summer. So you must order them at the beginning of summer if you want them in stock by then. It's a weird push-ahead world, especially for a store bearing shelves of books about living in the moment. "Find whatever Irish titles you can," Janet tells me. "Put them on a table up front. If there's anything you think we're lacking, order it."

45

I felt more than prepared for this first assignment, as I have a thing for Ireland. I was en route to my one and only trip to Poland when I first fell for a country to which I had not a single connection. I was halfway to Krakow, to where I'd spend the summer of 1976 on a full scholarship studying language and culture at Jagiellonian University, when my big white-and-blue Pan Am 740-something stopped in Shannon. Under the guise of the plane's needing fuel, we passengers asked to kill time in the terminal and drop money in the conveniently located duty-free gift shop. I spent a few bucks on a pendant bearing a piece of "lucky" Connemara marble, then spent the rest of the time staring out a rain-glazed window at landscape that seemed to be sucking me through the glass. I haven't made it back to Poland, but I returned to Ireland a dozen years later for my first visit outside the airport, and ten times since, walking, writing, eating enormous quantities of bread in a place that, despite growth and development, remains largely a world made solely of my favorite color. So this first display assignment at Janet's would be a no-brainer.

Pushing a two-shelved metal cart that glided along on two sets of squeaky wheels, I did a supermarket-sweep-type tour of the store. *The Lonely Planet Guide to Dublin* and *Best Irish Walks* from Travel, and on to History/Political Science for *The Great Hunger* and *How the Irish Saved Civilization.* Some Eavan Boland, Patrick Kavanaugh, and Seamus Heaney from Poetry/Reference/Drama and, from Classics, Joyce and Wilde. An Irish dictionary, cookbook, book of blessings. And from Fiction, O'Brien, McGahern, Healy, Boylan, and Colm Toibin's fat anthology with the gorgeous fine-grain cover photograph of a stone wall. I grabbed all the Roddy Doyles I could find because that is something I believe anyone who enters a bookstore ought to do. The fiction shelf held all his titles but one. *The Woman Who Walked into Doors* seemed to have run off.

"We need another book," I called over to Janet as I waved hands full of Paddy Clarkes and Henry Smarts, Snappers and Vans.

"Then let's order it," said Janet, drawing up to the computer one of the three pale green custom-made stools that were gifts from Edwardian daughter Margaret back when the store first opened. As a book is sold, Edwards' computer system, which goes by the frog-vocabulary name IBID, automatically places the name of that book on the list to be ordered the following day. Added to that list are the special orders people request, a title someone thinks might be popular due to its subject or the fact that it was written by a local author, or because of the season we're in or media attention. Add those we staffers want to see in the store. There is no central plan or preprogrammed mix that is ordered. Janet regularly scans online sources and publications including the *New York Times Book Review,* the *New York Review of Books, Publishers Weekly,* and *USA Today*'s Thursday book pages to make sure she has or will place on order the titles that sound most intriguing. The order must be transmitted by eleven A.M. in order to be delivered to Edwards in one or two days. In a store the size of this one, books are on the shelves by the end of the day the deliveryman rolls them in. Also by the end of the day, the call to tell people their special order is in has been placed.

Janet narrated for me the steps as her fingers slowly hit

the F7 F11 F8 F1 ENTER ESC combination with which you call up a title, then the order screen, and finally place the order. I typed in *Doyle,* then got a screen full of his titles, scrolled down to Woman (The very common title-starting word *The* is not used in this system), and selected her for ordering. I was pushing the keys here in downtown Springfield, Massachusetts, and this order would be filled by a huge warehouse in Pennsylvania operated at the time by Ingram, a huge national wholesaler of books and audiobooks to both enormous megastores and small ones like Edwards. Thus began my ride on the retail carousel that turns through all of the many possible gift-giving occasions on the calendar. Out back, a list taped to the wall gives the dates of the many events you could choose to celebrate in a single year. Along with biggies like Christmas and Hanukkah and Memorial Day and Thanksgiving are Earth Day and Grandparents' Day, along with something for everybody: Chinese Valentine's Day, International Forgiveness Day, Kewpie Doll Collector's Day. Each is a reason to showcase new and different merchandise. And anything new and different is better than old and the same. Especially when most of your clientele consists of the same folks day after day. They're going to see that same table of books day after day, unless you move things around. "I want this to be a different store every time someone comes in," Janet tells me. I see one table near the door. Twice as different, I figure, would be two. Twice the tables, twice the amount of merchandise.

"Could I add another table?"

"Right this way," Flo says, and directs me to clear a display of chewable board books in the Children's section.

She's happy and cheery and, I can tell, on my side. I'm glad to find Flo in my corner so immediately. Glad to find her at the store, period. She's had a nursing career, raised six kids (the last two of them twins), cofounded the bookstore, for seventeen years toiled from opening to closing, and is well past the traditional retirement age. So you might expect to see her face only on some sort of dusty commemorative-founder plaque nailed up in a corner, the real Flo ensconced in a Flo-ridian retirement village, feet up, umbrella drink in hand, best seller in lap. But it's Flo's face in real life, along with all five-feet-three of her, that you'll see at the store six days a week, from between nine or nine-thirty to four or four-thirty, Flo there, in black dress pants and black or red blazer, smile on her face and goodness in her nature, at the register, in the aisles, climbing up ladders, lugging boxes, pushing the squeaky book cart before going home to make some Italian specialty like polenta from scratch and feeding drop-in guests and family, then lifting a pair of weights to stave off osteoporosis and end her day.

Pure and simple, Flo was not a candidate for retirement. And, according to Janet, she is a huge reason the bookstore isn't, either. "Flo just flows" is how she puts it, recalling a lifetime of examples during which her mother's camel never had one too many straws. Childhood chicken pox, for instance. The six Edwards kids in five bedrooms, on each door a chart keeping track of who's had their temperature taken, who's had their medicine. Ever prepared, ever organized, there was Flo, handling everything.

"If organization is the key to success," Janet says, "she's what's kept us going."

Edwards is a second home for Flo and it's right across the river from her original one. Raised in West Springfield were Notre Dame's first Heisman Trophy winner, Angelo Bertelli; legendary baseball manager Leo Durocher; and Edwards' cofounder Flora Ferranti, whose parents had immigrated in the wave of northern Italians who came to this country just after 1900. Flo was four when her parents and two sisters and two brothers moved from their first home in Sagamore, on the Cape Cod Canal, to western Massachusetts and West Springfield, where an Italian enclave was burgeoning and railroad jobs were available. On the spot where the Ferranti family farm once stood, a neat row of brick apartments has been built. The wild land that was her playground across the street is now the one-hundred-seventy-five-acre Eastern States Exposition grounds, which every September is home to the "Big E," an enormous something-for-everybody fair attended by more than 1 million over its 17-day run. Over the years, Flo changed as well. Became a nursing student at what was Mary Hitchcock Hospital in Hanover, New Hampshire, now Dartmouth-Hitchcock Hospital, but still in Hanover, which is where Flo met Dartmouth student and future CPA Roy Edwards.

"There was nothing else in Hanover at the time," she tells me. "Just the hospital, and Dartmouth, which wasn't coed then. So he came up to the hospital. They all did. Because that's where all the females were."

Flo and Roy married in 1948, settled in his native Idaho, but returned to New Hampshire when Roy took a job with a construction firm. In 1958, when he became a partner in his own construction company, the family moved to Framingham, to a development of new houses with grass on one side and grass on the other, neighbors you knew on both sides, and plenty of room for those six kids. There were frequent trips to West Springfield, which Janet says always felt like home, and which she visited often during her years at the University of Massachusetts in nearby Amherst. "Grandparents, aunts, uncles, everybody was in West Springfield," she says. "Nobody besides my mother ever moved away."

And everybody was thrilled when Flo returned.

It was all because of books. In 1974, Roy's business partner suffered a heart attack that brought about the end of their construction business in Boston. Roy, then only fifty, began to look around for his next venture. Retail daredevil Marshall Smith had just begun to offer franchises of his Paperback Booksmith, which in 1961 became Boston's first all-paperback bookstore. Roy became one of the first franchisees, locating his store just north of Springfield, in the newly constructed Fairfield Mall right across from the Chicopee entrance to the Massachusetts Turnpike.

"The bookstore brought us back to western Massachusetts," says Flo between spoonfuls of cottage cheese eaten while she stands next to her computer. "My parents were still alive—it was almost like how Janet came back. A migration back to our roots, and to a new livelihood."

From her computer on the opposite side of the U-shaped counter, Janet gives the twist: "Mom and Dad sort of peeled off from the chain and became independent."

Marshall Smith would spend the next three decades filling what he saw as unmet needs. He founded a video chain (Videosmith), a home-learning chain (Learningsmith), and a computer-café chain (Cybersmith). All three businesses would fail. But his original bookstore, Brookline Booksmith, will turn forty-four in fall 2004 in the same 6,000-square-feet shop to which Smith moved in the midsixties, when its first home, 2,000 square feet a few doors down, proved insufficient. Located in a thriving retail neighborhood just steps from the busy Coolidge Corner subway stop in the village of Brookline, and staffed with genuine book lovers, it compounds those winning facts with a lively and near nightly series of readings in an adjacent basement space that once housed a grocery and now sees the likes of Saul Bellow holding forth where salami once was sliced. Add to all those facts how Brookline Booksmith nets virtually every huge author who's alive and breathing, orders daringly and ingeniously, and over the years has distributed an estimated 35,000 biscuits inside its canine-friendly doors (no count available on the number of gifts the pups might have given in return), and you start to understand why Brookline Booksmith consistently gets singled out at local and national award time.

If there were a prize for hiring, Brookline Booksmith would get that one, too.

As a shopper, I'm regularly disgusted by disconnected, distracted, disinterested, sometimes outright dissing clerks who give the definite impression they're doing me a favor by taking my money. That's never been the case during any of my many visits to the store (I did walk out one night, but only because of the boring delivery of a literary star I'd driven the ninety miles from my home to hear). Long before Janet knew my name, I felt welcome in her store as I returned the genuine hello she called out when I'd walk through the doors. I think of favorite bookstores in which I am not employed and consider what they have in common. The first three that spring to mind all happen to have restaurants, but there are reasons other than food for which I single them out. Staff, staff, staff, and, oh, staff. Nice staff. Staff that offer help, suggestions, can find what you're looking for, are able to suggest something else that might be along the same lines. Staff that also are customers. Who would be hanging around the store even if they weren't paid to. Not unlike characters in another British journalist's book—*High Fidelity* (1996), in which Nick Hornby dead-on details music-obsessed Peter Pans whose spiritual home is a vinyl record shop in London.

It's the same kind of gang on the payroll at a bookstore fifty-five miles east of Edwards, where, in a 27,000-square-foot brick factory that formerly housed the Sleeper & Hartley Manufacturing company—one of the world's leading manufacturers of spring-making equipment (their slogan was "The Machines That Put Rings In Springs")—twenty-nine-year-old Tatnuck Bookseller thrives. Sure, it lures customers via huge inventory, compelling discounts, a packed calendar of events, an ever-changing gift department, and a restaurant. But when I walk through those doors, the information desk is the first thing I see. And usually two smiling staffers greeting me—often Gloria

Abramoff, who co-owns the place along with husband and founder, Larry. Big smiles, big hello, big gratitude that you chose to come all the way down Chandler Street, in the exact opposite direction of the mammoth mall and its neighboring minicity of big chain stores. The first time I went through those doors, I also was greeted by Famous Amos of the eponymous cookie line. He was promoting a cookbook, standing just inside the front door and offering cookies, and greetings that were echoed by Gloria. Though they draw some of the bigger biggies, you might not meet one the instant you step inside. But you'll still remember your visit, because you were given regard. And you got the feeling that you'd want to return. After all, you ended up spending enough that you probably own a wing of the place.

Although clear across the country and located in quite the opposite setting—an eighteen-year-old 43,000-square-foot store attached to an upscale mall and overlooking a lake in Lexington, Kentucky—Joseph-Beth Booksellers inspires the same feeling. Miles of glass provide the most amount of natural light I've ever seen in a bookstore, brightness that flows to the lower level via an open plan that makes the top floor a very large balcony. Sure, there's an entire interactive music department, and next to Travel you will find a wide selection of luggage, and if that's not impressive enough, just past that, an actual travel agency is ready to help you book your tickets. The aforementioned restaurant includes a patio on the aforementioned lake, and after your feed you can relax by the fireplace, in leather-and-chrome chairs you just might find too comfortable to leave behind. If that's the case, just take out the wallet: the seats are for sale. There's plenty to keep you occupied—even before you pick up a single title—noted the pair of women who came to my signing there and announced they'd driven two hours. I was quite flattered—I don't know a soul in the entire state, and here were two readers who'd spend four hours in the car on this day, just for me. But it wasn't just for me. It was for Joseph-Beth. "Oh, we've never heard of you," they said, laughing, like that was funny or something. "We just knew there was going to be a reading, so we came for the day. Lunch, browsing, dinner, reading, dessert ... we love this store! We could live here!" I was there for work, but had time to kill beforehand, and came to agree with them as I browsed the shelves, ransacked the 50 percent–off cart, played with the CD listening stations. There was just an easy, pleasant, comfortable energy circling around the place, and when I heard my reading being announced, I almost felt disappointed that people were taking their seats.

OK, when I read at the Tattered Cover Book Store in Denver's Cherry Creek neighborhood I was given a bookmark with my name and reading date engraved on it. While it's cool to get personalized souvenirs, it was the staff that lit this place and made it memorable. I watched them, cheery and laughing, despite having to scale the sets of stairs between the building's three floors, plus an additional one to the top, where, on the night of my visit, the restaurant was hosting its own book event, a demo by an author-chef.

The store might stick in your mind even if you've never been anywhere west of the Mississippi. In early 2000, police demanded to search the purchase records of a customer who was a suspected drug manufacturer. Among evidence seized in an earlier raid on a mobile home in a nearby county was a methamphetamine lab, books on making the drug, and, in an exterior trash can, a book-shipping envelope and an invoice from the Tattered Cover Book Store. So police secured a search warrant for the invoice, and, in October, a Denver district judge ordered bookstore owner Joyce Meskis to release the document. She appealed the decision, and in April 2002 won a unanimous decision that recognized the rights of the public to purchase books anonymously without government interference.

"Had it not been for the Tattered Cover's steadfast stance, the zealousness of the City would have led to the disclosure of information that we ultimately conclude is constitutionally protected," Justice Michael Bender said in his decision. "Anonymity is a shield from the tyranny of the majority. It thus exemplifies the purpose behind the Bill of Rights, and of the First Amendment in particular: to protect unpopular individuals from retaliation—and their ideas from suppression—at the hands of an intolerant society."

Whatever your level of tolerance for the protection of methamphetamine manufacturers and dealers, put yourself in the shoes of the abovementioned criminal. What items might you have bought in your day that you wouldn't want made public? You might not have on your shelf the pair of how-to books listed on that receipt (*Advanced Techniques of Clandestine Psychedelic and Amphetamine Manufacturer*, by Uncle Fester—yes, correct author name—and *The Construction and Operation of Clan-*

destine Drug Laboratories, by Jack B. Nimble—ditto—but you might have a few skeletons in the closet of your own shopping history. Perhaps on your lunch hour you didn't stroll down to your version of Edwards, or Tatnuck, or the Tattered Cover to pick up the newest edition of *Pornography for Dummies,* but you might have keyed and clicked and in a few minutes had it ordered online for delivery to your door. Even if you read nothing more shocking than *Electronics Today,* your private business should remain just that.

Bruce Jones, the American Civil Liberties Union cooperating attorney who filed a brief in support of the bookstore, noted that the ruling was written "with a breath of analysis that will extend beyond just Colorado just because of how thorough and careful and persuasively the court presented its analysis."

A significant victory for what I almost was going to call "this little bookstore." Yes, there is that restaurant— and have I mentioned the multistory parking garage? However, the fact that the Tattered Cover is an independent—it opened in 1971 and Meskis bought it three years later—makes it precious—seemingly small (40,000 square feet now but it started out at 950) in these dot-com-bookstore days. Whatever the actual dimensions, its win for the rights of the alleged druggie is, really, a victory for you. Whatever you buy. Wherever you shop.

Edwards included.

Even without court edict, there's a confidentiality observed at that bookstore desk. It's a combination of patient/physician-don't-ask-don't-tell, and it's common courtesy. There are loads of books on abuse and disease here, giving Edwards something in common with the downstairs CVS. Lots of stock of a personal nature. Books and magazines on medical conditions, emotional turmoil, legal tangles, and enough material of a sexual nature. Your selecting a title on abortion or bankruptcy, divorce or gender change, is, and should be, your business. When I first began at the store, I got into the habit of handing over change with the wish "Enjoy your *Newsweek!*" or "Enjoy your *Fix-It-and-Forget-It Cookbook!*" Then I took the $6.95 for *How to Survive the Loss of a Love* and realized I probably should just say thanks and 'bye.

But it's still just my first day on the job at Edwards, and a woman comes in to pick up the two books she'd ordered: Two, count 'em, two copies of *The Dual Disorders Recovery Book.* The special orders are filed by surname, so Pat asks her for that. The customer volunteers her name, the title, and the total number requested. There is the springboard for a host of "hey, covering all the bases" type of comments, but Pat simply says, "Here you are," without adding, as I might be tempted to, "One for each of you!" She takes the money, bags the purchase, and the woman leaves. I wait for a crack from Pat. But she only neatens the special-order shelf and takes a seat on one of the short little stools.

I know Pat only from my visits to the store, where she stands out due to her long, straight India-ink black hair and a colorful wardrobe that pops against Janet's and Flo's preferred black. Pat has a cool selection of earrings, too, many of them beaded and reflecting her Native American heritage. She always has been cordial to me, and I prod her now to see if we possibly might share a vein for joking.

"You gotta love that she wanted two copies," I say. Pat smiles. I continue poking. "You must see all types. . . ."

"You do."

She doesn't say anything else.

Then she does. "As much as you'd like to say something at times, you don't," she tells me. "I learned a long time ago not to comment on what people are buying." Pat stands up to take the $3.99 for a copy of *Cat Fancy*. Continues on to tell me that she's sensitive to body language and can tell when customers looks nervous about their purchases. If they do, Pat says nothing, or might try to lighten them up.

"If they're buying a travel book, I'll say 'Have a nice trip.' But if it's something on divorce, a kind of book like that, I don't say anything."

She credits the store for that finesse, says it's taught her a lot about herself and about how she interacts. Connecting with others is a challenge for the woman who grew up an only child until age twelve. The added sibling was a boy, and a natural in her all-boy neighborhood.

"I learned how to be alone," Pat says. "And that's still my preference."

Her previous job in an office setting didn't help. The last few years there were negative, and she dealt with that by pushing others away, more than obviously letting them know that she didn't want to be bothered.

"I had to get past that. The store kind of helped me. It's a place that will give you an education. I don't make friends easily, can't call myself a social person. I don't go out and interact all that much. The people I work with, I like. It pretty much satisfies any emotional need I might have for interaction. The personalities are hugely varied, the customers, the regulars who come in ... and I've gotten so now I can banter back and forth, no matter what the person's profession is. Judges, or other clerks, street people even. So it's really kinda cool to be interacting, and knowing people from such varied walks of life."

It's just after one. The lunchtime rush ends around one thirty, as does Pat's workday. Many would love to have their shift completed just as the afternoon has begun and *The Bold and the Beautiful* is about to start. But Pat does not have a schedule I covet, mainly because she has to wake at a single-digit hour. Edwards' business day is keyed to that of the downtown work community that is the store's main customer base. Therefore, doors must be open and fresh newspapers stacked at the ready by seven thirty A.M., when the office world begins it own waking process. This means Pat's up at four thirty.

She's a morning person, a plus considering the hour at which her alarm rings. Pat tells me she'd prefer six A.M., then adds, "But I say 'What the heck.' That gets me here for quarter of seven, enough time not to rush. I try to keep chaos out of my life as much as possible."

Heck would not be the particular curse I'd be using at four thirty A.M., so more power to Pat, who takes the morning in stride, having the store prep down to a science. She pulls the squeaky cart onto the slow freight elevator down the hall and takes it two floors down, to the garage of Tower Square, to retrieve the stacks of newspapers left at two separate loading docks. Then it's back upstairs to swap yesterday's news for today's, pull the copies reserved by customers, turn on the computers and the various credit card and other electronic gizmos, and ready the counter for opening.

"It's a nice pace in the morning," she says. "I put the music on, groove to that before I open the doors."

Pat's job is a crucial one. No Pat there at seven thirty A.M., no doors open at seven thirty A.M., no morning buzz of people in and out, most of them to buy papers, but point is, people coming in, the day's business starting. The store carries the city's sole daily, *The Union-News,* which sits high and proud on its own white plastic newsstand. To the left of that is a set of shelves bearing, at the top, the hottest magazines, including *Time, Newsweek, New York,* the *New Yorker, Forbes,* the *Economist, Entertainment Weekly, In Touch, Us, Sports Illustrated,* and *People.* Below those are two shelves of the rest of the daily newspapers: the *Boston Globe, Boston Herald, New York Times, New York Post, New York Daily News, Hartford Courant, USA Today, Investor's Business Daily.* Numbers stocked daily range from forty copies of the *Union-News* down to three *Investor's Business Daily.* Along with greeting cards and magazines, the papers are important inventory. The profit margin is extremely slim—approximately twelve cents on a fifty-cent paper—but they get people in the door.

As do those magazines, on which the store makes no more than 20 percent of the cover price. The popular titles are displayed on the end cap of a long set of white shelves, both sides lined with periodicals for most every conceivable legal interest.

To the right, women stand in front of *Fit Pregnancy, Prom, Girlfriend, Self, More, Vogue, Soap Opera Weekly, La Cucina Italiana, What's for Dinner, Good Housekeeping, Real*

Simple, Bath and Kitchen, Elle Decor, Black Tress, Black Hair, Hot Hair, Bridal Star Hairstyle, Bridal Guide, Weddings.

The crafty flip through *Stitchery World, Tole World, Stamp It, Country Afghans, Threads.* Across from them, the hip snap up *Interview, Rolling Stone, Movieline, Premiere.* Musicians in town for performances get armloads of *Guitar World, Modern Drummer, Revolver, Jazz Time, Blender, The Source, Spin, Latin Beat,* and I know this because when you wait on somebody with six or eight music magazines I don't think it's snooping to ask if he or she plays an instrument. With the local ethnic communities in mind, Pat keeps the shelves current with *People en Español, Essence, Ebony, Heart & Soul, Black Men Magazine, O, Savoy, Sister 2 Sister,* and, for the good-natured guy who works at the hotel and always hopes he gets upstairs before they're sold out, *Jet.*

The after-school crowd, or parents with flu patients who stayed home today, will head for *Disney Magazine, Star Trek the Magazine, Word Up, Power, Toy Fare, Pop Star, Ignite, Kid Planet, Slam, Tuff Stuff.* Businesspeople from the Tower want *Yachting, National Fisherman, Ocean Navigator, Golf for Women, Climbing Gear Guide, Backpacker, American Angler.* I've yet to see (though I really have no desire to), the reader who comes in for *Fur-Fish-Game.*

Janet's not a censor, but there's not much on the shelves that would shock. The only thing behind the counter in a paper bag is another leftover from Donald and John. Nor does she order copies of the *National Enquirer* and the *News of the World.* So if you're looking for graphic nudity or the Bush twins' alien love children, you'll have to search elsewhere.

Even so, an alarmingly large number of males un-abashedly ask for fantasy. They're not walking away with *Playboy* or *Caribbean Elbow Fetishist*—they seek entire publications devoted to the assembly and maintenance of made-up baseball and football teams over which they will obsess for an entire sporting season. *Rotowire Fantasy Baseball, New Extra Fantasy Baseball, The Fantasy Baseball Guide: Professional Edition* await them—and the occasional female competitor—in a section of the magazine aisle I like to call Man Land. Overbrimming with testosterone are *Baseball Digest, Preview Sports, ESPN the Magazine, Masters of Karate, Black Robe, FightSmart, Runner's World, Health and Fitness, Muscle, Fitness Workout, IronmanInside, Triguide, Men's Health, Stuff, King, FHM, Ramp, Maxim, GQ, Black Book, Details, CycleWorld, Motorcycle Cruiser, Popular Mechanics, Road and Track, Compact Car, Hemmings Motor News, Car and Driver Buyers Guide to Pick-Ups, Sport-Utilities and Vans.*

This selection morphs into the unisex:

Kiplinger's Mutual Funds, Money 'n Profits, Start Your Own Business, Get Rich at Home, Smart Computing, Pocket PC, PC Basics, PC Photo, Outdoor Photographer, Digital Photographer, Computer Videomaker, Video Buyer's Guide, which blast into the space occupied by *Astronomy, Sky and Telescope, Smithsonian, Popular Science, The Environmental Magazine, Natural New England, Scientific American, Psychology Today, Mad, Artist Magazine,* and *Writer's Digest.*

Every Thursday, a distributor delivers six to eight huge magazine-packed Tupperware-like red-and-blue crates called totes. Inside are the freshest periodicals, ready for reading. By the end of the following day, Pat has completed the job of replacing old issues with new, and keeping inventory of it all. The outdated copies go back into the totes, and count toward credit. "I pull out whatever we didn't sell for that month," she tells me, "just to keep the inventory down. The average cost of a magazine is four dollars and ninety-five cents, but some of the magazines these days are nine and ten dollars. Especially kids' magazines. It blows my mind, but the kids spend the money on them. Or they just come in and read them. . . ."

That's usually in the quieter afternoon, or after-school, hours, long after Pat's gone home, when the store's two busiest points of the day are over and she's done dealing with the most rushed customers: those en route to their workdays, or those taking too-quick breaks at lunch. As Pat once did, when she came to the store as a shopper.

When Pat told me more about her last workplace, I was struck again how the bookstore seems to be a refuge, and one for women. Roy is there daily to do the picky paperwork required for the returning of newspapers, and he'll haul trash and flattened cardboard down to the compactors. But all that's done out of sight. A sisterhood is the face of this store.

Pat was an Edwards customer for her nearly twenty-five years of work in a downtown office. She enjoyed the job until a new partner joined the firm. His personality increased the stress level, and her blood pressure. Her leave was sudden, and rather dramatic: "I said, 'I can't deal with this any more.' And I left. Quit on the spot. I kind of totally freaked out."

She was given the opportunity to return to her job, if she'd only apologize for some comments made in the parting act. She refused. "I went for three or four months without any work at all, which I needed. But I couldn't afford it. I just kind of walked in the store one day and asked, 'You need any help?' Janet hired me. That was seven years ago, and I've been here ever since."

As I once did during my downtown workdays, Pat used to patronize both Johnson's and Edwards.

"I'm a reader, and I always go for the new books—I've read the rest of them," she said. "And after a while at Johnson's, I found out that most of their new books came in later than anybody else's. Little by little I started shopping more here. I got to know Janet fairly well—as well as you can know somebody from coming in and buying a product and leaving. I felt fairly confident, when I went in and asked for work, that if she had space she'd hire me. I kept looking around, put resumes out. But I didn't want another office job. Edwards initially was temporary—until I found something better. And I never did. I just stopped looking."

I'm glad Pat stopped. We need her kind here. The type that thinks it's kinda cool to help customers. To give the all-too-often uncommon common courtesy. Today's bookstores face new and increased competition, and this one's no exception. It also faces the dim corridor of a half-empty mall. Look out the double doors and into the mall space and you'll see vacant storefronts to your left and right. Across the way, there are signs of life in Cheraine's, which deals in collectible statuettes of pop characters like Pluto and Mickey. To the left of that are the lights of the newly redesigned food court. But other than that, in this corner of the second floor of Tower Square, all is still.

* * *

It was a different story—a different place complete with a different name—in 1982, when a local newsstand was closing in downtown Springfield, and Roy and Flora saw an opportunity to bring Edwards to the mall then known as Baystate West. In the '60s, federal aid for urban renewal projects fueled efforts to revitalize a downtown that, like so many others throughout the Northeast, had seen better days. Standing twenty-nine stories—twenty-one of them office space—the tower was designed by Eduardo Catalano, for whom cement must have held special appeal. Tons of it make up Baystate West/Tower Square and his other two nearby creations, the Hall of Justice and the Civic Center. Baystate West became the city's tallest structure, towering over the first to hold that title, the three-hundred-foot-tall Campanile that is a replica of the one in Venice's St. Mark's Square. Containing the twelve-bell Municipal Chimes that no longer ring, it is located between City Hall and Symphony Hall, a pair of Parthenon-ish buildings that critics rightfully have called among the most beautiful in the nation.

It would never fit into that category, but Baystate West was noteworthy for initially living up to its purpose: attracting crowds for reasons other than the curious airwalk that spanned Main Street from the mall to the second floor of Steiger's, Springfield's very own and much-beloved department store. At that time, the mall contained fifty-five stores. Downtown was hopping. When the Edwardses moved the business from Chicopee, independent bookstores were as viable as the bank. Johnson's was doing booming business.

"But talk about dying by a thousand cuts." Janet is describing the downturn. "You look at the small deteriorations one by one and a trickle becomes a flood and of course when Holyoke Mall began to expand, there was a sucking sound as life went out of Main Street. And it wasn't just Springfield. Look at Holyoke, Chicopee. Mrs. Sharpe."

I look. I can't see Holyoke and Chicopee from here (unfortunately, other than the big plate-glass walls flanking the entrance, there are no windows in Edwards), but I can see a smiling woman at the counter, sifting through a purse and counting out fifty cents in change.

"This is Mrs. Sharpe," Janet tells me, and I say what I'm thinking, which is, "What a great name." She answers that she thinks she has a nickel in here somewhere. I don't say my next thought, which is that I'm going to steal her name in the way I often steal names for my stories, including one I swiped from the newspaper's bridal section years back: Mrs. Joe Dull. As Janet puts away the change given by Mrs. Sharpe, I laugh to myself, remembering an outdoor book signing the spring before at A Novel Idea in my neighboring Belchertown. A woman and her entourage had walked up for an introduction: "I'm Mrs. Joe Dull. This is my Dull mother-in-law, and these are my Dull children."

Janet hands Mrs. Sharpe her reserved papers. I work to focus. Check my watch. I realize I have missed my nap. A first in maybe seven months.

"The question is not why all the other stores have gone

black," Janet is continuing. "The question is, Why are the lights still on at Edwards Books?"

I look around. It's early afternoon. There are maybe three people in the store. She's asked a good question, and answers it. Says that it's not about money. It's about quality of life, an expression she says she hates, but believes that in this case, it fits.

"To have a hands-on personal relationship—not with customers, but with friends, with the neighborhood. It's not just 'Hi, how are you?' You see what goes on downtown. The crazies, the funnies, the friends, the really good people. This is like—I don't know—this is living. There are frustrations, but the payback in friendships is immeasurable. It's the feeling of being supported. The feeling of being together in this."

Janet points to H PS—History/Political Science—the shelves where you'll find the 2000 best seller *Bowling Alone: The Collapse and Revival of American Community*, in which self-described "obscure academic" Robert Putnam explores an American society disconnecting from family, friends, neighborhoods, and even its own country.

"There is a feeling of isolation today, that community doesn't happen," Janet's saying. "It really is a world begging for connection. And you don't have to look very far to find it. It's unbelievable what happens when people come through those doors. Maybe community is lacking elsewhere, but here, in this store, sometimes we know too much about one another." Without missing a beat, and because she knows too much about me, Janet continues: "Shouldn't you be going home?" I shrug.

"Then let me get you something to eat," she says.

"No, that's OK...."

"You, too, can be overworked and underpaid, but we'll feed you." She pulls a ten from the drawer. "What do you want?"

And thus begins the big continuous march to various Tower Square eating establishments, from which I will be fed by a boss who not only pays for whatever I want but schleps out to get it for me. Tea and a blueberry scone, usually. Or a hubcap-size oatmeal-raisin cookie. But if it's a longer day, she counts me in for a veggie burger, a falafel, a slice of the pizza Christina's getting, or the fries for which eventually is stocked a bottle of Heinz 57 wearing a homemade sticker "Corporate Ketchup." If we get hungry in between any of these feeds, Flo has a bag of pretzels near her computer, and in a drawer just to the right of that, a secret chocolate stash that gets restocked by an anonymous purchaser of giant-sized Hershey's with almonds.

Right now, I'm not staying simply for the food. I'm staying because I want to see what UPS has brought. Twice a day, morning and early afternoon, books are delivered to the store. A third delivery is possible some days, but normally it's two, the second of which on my first day is ferried in by the young UPS guy with the brown uniform and the cheery personality. He sets three boxes on the floor on Flo's side of the counter, asks her to sign his computerized receipt holder. Before he leaves, he has a wish for us: "Have a sparkling day!"

Flo waves me toward the back room and says, "I'll show you how to receive."

The last two lines sound very cosmic. So I'm not going anywhere. Cautioning me that I shouldn't be picking up anything heavy, Flo hefts the boxes onto the squeaky cart and rolls them into the back room, parking them in front of a set of shelves. The top shelf is a collection of water bottles, scrap paper, clipboards, and mugs holding pens and pencils, and, as you move to the right, you're all set for personal care items. Hand cream. Hairspray. Band-Aids. Toothpaste. Mouthwash. Tampons. Hairbrush, selection of ponytail holders, that set of electric curlers. The five shelves below bear thin paper labels that yell FOR RECEIVING ONLY and are effective, seeing how the Advil and Midol and all the rest have steered clear of taking up any space there. Flo and I will be receiving. The lower shelves are for us.

From one of the pen mugs, Flo picks out a box cutter like the ones I used in that meat-wrapping job back in high school. She slits the single line of plastic tape that holds the first carton closed. Beneath is more plastic, clear and sucked of air to conform to the lump of books beneath and prevent them from shifting en route. Flo makes another long stab and tears the plastic back with the enthusiasm I once used in ripping open the foil from childhood pans of Jiffy Pop. You can understand the anticipation. Even though the order was placed by this store, and even though, somewhere in one of these three boxes, an invoice tells you exactly what's in them, there's still a buzz about reaching inside and pulling out fresh new stories. Covers pristine, pages yet to be open or marked by pen or wrinkle, spines straight and uncracked.

At the top of the pile in the carton is the face of Peter Greenberg, who I know as the *Today* show's travel expert.

This is his current best seller, *The Travel Detective: How to Get the Best Service and the Best Deal from Airlines, Hotels, Cruise Ships, and Car Rental Agencies.* I lift a stack of four of him to find four of Jimmy Carter's *An Hour before Daylight: Memories of My Rural Boyhood.* Beneath Peter and Jimmy, a fat basement: rows and endless levels to the bottom of the box, all the same title: *1st to Die: A Novel,* by James Patterson.

"Oh—Patterson," Flo says, and removes *1st to Die* after *1st to Die,* separating them on the empty shelves from the *Rural Boyhood,* which is separated further from the *Travel Detective.* I'm told to stack the books by category, by the sections of the store for which they're bound. All dictionaries together, all young-adult novels together, all travel, all biography, all mass-market paperbacks, which are the beachy fat kind as opposed to the slimmer, larger trade versions.

We slit the second box and begin to remove the contents, a process Flo abandons as she tells me, "We have to remember to check for specials," and disappears back into the store.

I look at the shelves. There's an instructional on coaching youth soccer. A cookbook of all things lemon. Several installments in a series called *The Magic Treehouse,* which looks like it's for kids but sounds like a high school hangout for the kind of boys your mother warned you about.

"They all look special to me," I tell Flo, who returns holding a fat stack of paper slips.

It turns out that the *Totally Lemons Cookbook* is a special—a special order—as are two of the Jimmy Carters, one of the Pattersons, and a fat directory of nothing but Italian verbs. The papers bearing the customer's name get slid into the correct books and those books get brought out to the counter and placed next to the phone so one of us can dial the customers with the news that their books have arrived. Somewhere out there, Italian verbs are needed. As is knowledge of the proper technique for reaming. Somebody out there wants to be the first on the block with *1st to Die,* while another is longing for the inside dope on Miss Lillian and Billy. It's the whole *Healing the Heart* thing. These specials are special to somebody.

In the final box, we find the invoice. Six five-by-seven sheets on which the books in these three boxes are listed alphabetically. There are four pages of books we have been sent, and a page and a half of ones we haven't. Those have the unfortunate designation of BO, which, in bookstore-speak, simply means backorder, OS for out of stock, OSI for out of stock indefinitely, NSI for not in stock, or OP, the very sad out of print. We check off those that have arrived, then walk over to Flo's computer, where we must now hit numerous digits and F keys in order to bring up this invoice online and acknowledge that we indeed have received. The new books then officially will be in the system. Flo explains this last process to me as she goes along, but she's losing me. I'm horrible with numbers. Didn't I tell Janet that?

But I worry for nothing. The work is quick and it's done! Now a new task—to put the books on the correct shelves. Flo volunteers, asking me to watch the register until Janet comes back from picking up the reason she moved to Springfield after sixteen years in Brooklyn.

Suzanne Strempek Shea

* * *

Twenty minutes later, twenty feet ahead of her mother, in strides eleven-year-old Christina Rose, fresh from her day of seventh grade at the city's Chestnut Accelerated Middle School. I remember first seeing her behind the counter years back, when she was in parochial-school plaid and wore her straight brown hair down to her waist. It's not as long now but still falls past her shoulders, and denim is her choice now that she has her choice of school attire. Her face is still Renaissance seraphim, oval, pale, with large brown eyes that widen when she greets me and unburdens her shoulder of an enormous schoolbag-backpack that is the canvas for numerous penned doodles and names.

Being brought to the bookstore is Christina's daily after-school routine, another arc in the full circle that begins with the morning lift to school by her mother. The next destination, in another four hours or so, will be home.

Christina places her first bookstore memory at around the age of six. She was at her grandparents' home, not feeling well and, like any little kid in that situation, she wanted her mother.

Roy brought her in, and she stayed.

Most of her classmates hop off the bus and head for the TV, the computer, the phone. Christina essentially heads to a workplace. Expecting a moan? Get ready for a positive review. "I like the openness," she tells me. "The way that anyone can come in. Just about everyone who comes in here my mom knows and I know. There's that familiarity from coming here all my life. I wouldn't consider my childhood a normal one. I've grown up around thirty-five-

73

and forty-year-old doctors and lawyers. I was reading at such a young age, have had that influence of reading, of the family being in here. It's almost a safe haven."

There's no computer at home, so Christina cherishes her time at the Hewlett Packard next to the register. But first she must do her homework. She might be seated behind the counter, but Christina isn't expected to wait on customers unless no one else is available. When she must, she does so with energy and cordiality, easily making recommendations, and change.

Christina likes to tell the story of a friend who walked into the store and was shocked to find her at the register.

"She says 'Christina! What are you doing here?' I said, 'My mom owns the store.' 'How does she own a bookstore?' She didn't think it was possible to own a store. I think it's cool. How could you not have fun in a bookstore?"

"I didn't tell her to say that!" Janet swears, and, as she pulls out some paper money for Christina's after-school snack, she tells me of her previous life, when she returned to her work as a recruiter following Christina's birth. Her Brooklyn-to-Manhattan commute, despite being only twelve miles, lasted one hour on even the express bus. She was lucky if she got to the city in fifty-five minutes.

Without a plan, her decision to leave the city evolved when Roy was facing hip surgery and Flo needed assistance at the store.

"I had finally given up the job in the city and had taken that summer to decide what I was going to do," Janet says. "I came to spend two weeks—at least what I thought

would be about two weeks—at my mom's and was helping her in the bookstore. To see your child in the grass in
the backyard ... I suppose you want to bring your child
up the way you were brought up. If you were brought up
in Manhattan, that life might seem right to you. I was
brought up in a single-family home with grass on one side,
grass on the other side, neighbors we knew. It was just
more comfortable here."

But Janet had loved New York. Had loved her
recruiting job. "I never expected to come back and do
this," she tells me. "But a child will change your whole
perspective."

"Ain't that the truth."

Another country heard from. Another mother. Katrina
Deragon, Mom to two, and the one Edwards staffer I'd yet
to encounter on this day. Katrina often has joined Janet to
sell books at events I've done locally, so I know her a bit,
as I know her humor, which is taller than she. And that's
saying something because Katrina's five-ten, and likes to
wear heels.

She's another one big on black clothing, big black
handbag, and silver jewelry, only she wears lots of the latter. Several rings, bracelets, pins at once, to a dazzling effect. She's working at a nearby bank, and has just stopped
in. Which is how she got her bookstore job in the first
place.

"I would come in as a patron, and then one morning,
probably a month or so before Christmas, forty-eight years
ago, I saw Janet at the mezz getting breakfast" is how Katrina remembers it. "She said she was shorthanded. Did I
want to work a little? So here I am."

The actual calculation is five years since Katrina said yes, and started on weekends, then added some afternoons, which she's working now, the tail end of the day, including the all-important closing of the machines and the locking up of everything, which allows Janet and Christina to leave for home earlier.

Katrina likes dealing with books, sharing other book lovers' company, and attending any kind of book event. An aspiring journalist, she says simply, "Being around words is an inspiration. I especially like looking at the advance reader books. Getting a leg up on stuff. I've worked less and more, I've had time in and out. I'm like a bad penny. But it's like you end up at the bookstore for one reason or another, and something just makes you stay."

Until quitting time, at least, which is what this is for Flo, who has put on a white windbreaker and is holding her black handbag and pink-foam lunch cooler that she identifies for me as Christina's old *Baywatch* Barbie lunch bag from about the third grade. After that info she says, "OK, kiddo, I'm going home. Why don't you, too?"

"I will," I say. Though we're both forty-two, Katrina has a presence that normally reduces me to the humor level half the age of Christina, and I feel myself craving the opportunity for a good laugh. I don't yet want to leave, so I give Flo a hug good-bye. She's just a little taller than my collarbone. She hugs back. She's strong.

"Want to come for polenta?" she asks, then answers herself: "No, no, you go home. Go home and rest. Janet? Polenta?"

"We'll be there."

* * *

The store is late-afternoon quiet. Janet opens the blue vinyl binder that is her checkbook. Dials the bank's automated system and starts to do her balancing. Christina is online, working hard on some site that allows you to make cyber paper dolls. A few men stand and read magazines in the general vicinity of Sports. The other line rings from the back room and Janet yells, "Line two!" which means to grab the portable phone just past the girl making the paper dolls. Katrina gets there first, and says to the caller, "Let me look that up for you," before taking a seat at Janet's computer.

I'll get a rain check on the laugh. I'm suddenly feeling ready to head home to my own version of polenta. In my first day at the bookstore, I have worked six and a half hours. Five and a half more than I expected I'd feel up to.

I find my coat on its hook out back. The shelves for receiving still hold books that need putting away. I grab a stack of travel directories to places I've never been. Not just descriptions of restaurants and places of interest, but maps, too. Big, unfoldable guides of the type you need when you wake up and find yourself in a new strange world. Before I head out the door, I make sure I file them correctly, the Portugal under P and the South Africa under—well, would that be S or A? I want them to be in the right place. Because I want people to be able to find them. Because on this day that I started finding my way out of the woods, I can say that I know it is no fun to feel lost.

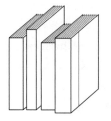

HE DOESN'T WANT TO BE HERE. YOU CAN TELL.
He shifts in place and breathes tensely, as if his olive
military-dress uniform with its prim tie and colorful pins
suddenly has shrunk a couple of sizes. But I know it's just
that he doesn't want to be here, in the Self-Help aisle. Like
so many men before him, he asks for a lifeline.

"Excuse me," he whispers, when I walk past spe-
cifically because I know he's not finding what he needs.
"I'm looking for a book. . . ."

"Yes?"

"On . . ." He knows what he wants, but how to put it?
"On talking, to, you know, women."

He makes it sound like he needs to communicate with
a faraway tribe, and I am tempted to lead him over to the
Foreign Languages section. Instead, I tell him he's come
to the right place. I gesture to the section of shelves right

in front of him. He looks straight ahead to the top one, which a paper sign designates as the place for books on DIVORCE. *The Massachusetts Women's Divorce Handbook; Mom's House, Dad's House: Making Two Homes For Your Child;* and my personal favorite of the titles there, and possibly in the entire store, *Joint Custody with a Jerk.* The man says "no" because that's jumping ahead. There's a long way to go between wanting to talk to a woman to having to talk with her legal representatives. His eyes shoot to the left, to the shelf marked Recovery. Melody Beatty and all her wisdom to help you be *Codependent No More.* Alcoholics Anonymous handbooks with cover drawings of stairways. Pocket-size affirmation books for the food-addicted, the self-esteemless, the overstressed.

"Next shelf down," I direct him, and I point to *Dating for Dummies. Body Language Secrets: A Guide during Courtship & Dating. Don't Be Afraid to Ask: How to Date a Beautiful Woman.* Somehow, a paperback titled *Dating Old Photographs* has been shelved there. Except for that last book, this shelf holds all the information he could ever need.

But maybe not. "No," he repeats. "Not dating. Talking. Talking. How should I talk to them? Is there a book like that?"

"Let me get Janet."

Janet knows all. Sees all. Reads just about all. Pick a category, a set of shelves, grab a book from random and chances are she can tell you chapter and verse. Of her favorites, she can even recite the first few lines, something she'll do off the cuff as she introduces an author at a reading. She polishes off two books in a weekend. And then there's those five nights in between. Janet has disconnected the TV at home, an attempt to divert Christina's attention more toward her schoolwork. So at night, behind the pink front door of their off-white three-bedroom ranch in the city's East Forest Park neighborhood ten minutes from the store, it's a scene straight out of Laura Ingalls Wilder's *Little House on the Prairie*. The night is passed with a pair of chromosomally related noses pressed to books.

All that arms both Janet and Christina with plenty of suggestions for those in search of a good story. And if you don't like what they recommend, bring it back. No questions asked. Janet started that policy when she joined the staff in 1991, and since then only three recommended books have been returned by readers. As long as it was suggested to you by a staff member—from Christina on up to Flo—you can return it. If you picked it out yourself and you hate it, well, you can always donate it to my library's bookstore.

I've worked at Janet's a month at this point, and already can't count the number of times I've seen her place a book in a reader's hands and say, "If you don't like it, bring it back." When I asked if she learned the recommending practice from her folks, she told me she got it from a pair of women she knew only as the bookmobile ladies.

"I'm another bookmobile child," she tells me, and we high-five. I feel all the more part of a cool community when she asks if I know that Stephen King also is. Two states to the south of King's, the young Edwards family all those years ago found an unexpected perk to their new home in Framingham:

"We got a split level, and we got a bookmobile stop right out front," Janet beams. "On Thursdays, after school, around three thirty or four. It was my ambition to read every book in the bookmobile. Nobody clued me in that they kept restocking the shelves. We moved there when I was seven. By age twelve, I had that figured out."

The two librarians were straight from central casting, with cat-eyeglasses and sweaters draped over the shoulders and held with pearly clips, the ownership of which became another goal for Janet. Other than fashion sense and plenty to read, the librarians also gave her the intimate gift of knowing just what would appeal to her.

"I'm only thinking about this now—it never occurred to me—that sense of wonder. From time to time one of them would say, 'Oh, Janet, we found something that would be perfect for you.' I'm seven or eight years old and I'm being shown that someone cares enough about me that she would put aside a book with my name on it. How could I do anything but become a fanatic about putting the right book into the right hands, if that was my experience, if that was my model? Here were these women and I remember them giving me *Black Beauty, Jane Eyre,* and, as the time became appropriate, Beverly Cleary, Henry Huggins, Homer Price. It's almost like I can be right back in the bookmobile, stepping onto those steps, and hearing, 'Oh, Janet, we've got just the book for you!' Maybe that's what I've been trying to do here. Because that was like the best thing that ever happened to me."

I think of my own bookmobile ladies: Mrs. Bigda, Mrs. Rehor, my mother. I wonder if they ever realized that, while out on their rounds, they were delivering more than a selection of books.

Long before it became a film, *The English Patient* was the initial book Janet matched to a reader. The first time she really listened to what the customer was looking for, she found herself saying, "Try this, I think you're going to like it. This is a book you really should read."

"I was waiting to recommend it to somebody because it's not a mainstream book that you're going to give to everybody. I was waiting to say, 'This is a beautiful novel. Read this book!' Close on the heels of that was Jonathan Harr's *A Civil Action*, long before it became popular. There are so many attorneys in the store, I thought, if it went well...."

Through Janet, the good acts by that pair of librarians have trickled down to unknown numbers of readers. The latest being the man who wants to talk to women, the man who, when Janet takes over the case, tells her that it's not all women he wants to talk to, but a specific one.

"I've found the right one," he says. "I just don't want to make a mistake."

Janet points to *Men Are from Mars, Women Are from Venus*. But he mistakenly zeroes in on the adjacent title, *Mars and Venus in the Bedroom,* and that's when he assures her, "Oh, no—everything's going great in the bedroom and all. I just want to talk to her."

This man, for whom Janet ultimately suggests something called *The Five Languages of Love,* is one of the many she's helped in the aisle that is one side take-me-away fiction and the other side in-your-face reality. As you enter, to your left are shelves of Psychology and Parenting, to your right is Fantasy, and the L through Z of mass-market paperbacks. So you'll have some guy thumbing through *Wizard's First Rule (Sword of Truth, Book 1)* and backing into a woman who's sniffling through the table of contents in *The Intimacy Factor: The Ground Rules for Overcoming the Obstacles to Truth, Respect, and Lasting Love.* To the sniffling, Janet brings further recommendations, and a box of Kleenex. I've seen her escort overemotional strangers into the back room, where she shuts the door, and there, among the fax machine and the electric curlers and the cart of flattened cardboard boxes, she listens as they tell her how difficult their lives are, their situations, their jobs, their parents, their lovers, their children. Janet can say, "I know" to much of this, and actually mean it. She knows the lot of the modern woman, the overworked woman, the underpaid woman, the single-parenting woman, the woman in general. Many of us do. But if we also had a billion other things to do in our day, how many of us would be hauling some sobbing stranger into a private counseling session?

"Where's the woman with the long hair?" a man asks me. "With the glasses? She helped me last time I was in Springfield. A year ago. I want to say thanks. I brought my wife in to meet her."

The wife nods. I don't know where Janet is. The store isn't that big, she has to be here somewhere. Then I see her, in the corner where Sports meets Computers. She's chatting with a woman, holding in one hand a four-inch-thick directory of American schools and colleges, and in the other, *Empty Nest, Full Heart: The Journey from Home to College.*

Some of Edwards customers are pilots and flight attendants on layover from Bradley International Airport, which is twenty minutes south in Windsor Locks, Connecticut. All are very polite, well groomed, often with Southern accents, usually dressed in Hawaiian shirts or sweat suits that look definitely after hours-ish. They buy many copies of *Around the World in a Bad Mood,* a humorous look at their everyday reality; they buy paperback fiction and lots of magazines; some of the women stock up on big photograph-heavy books by TV-show decorators, to plan for the changes they want to make at home whenever they finally get a chance to spend some time there. Often these visitors end up in Psychology. The section, that is. Because even those of us who look put together and relaxed have the problems the disheveled fast-lane rest of us might: raising teenage girls, managing finances, dealing with parents afflicted by Alzheimer's, determining whether to stay in a relationship, wondering if we're on the correct life path, finding downtime for ourselves so we can think about all that stuff—and can actually read the books on the subjects. One afternoon, a pilot came looking for something on rekindling love. He actually said that: "Do you have a book on rekindling love?" Instantly I could see the little fire inside a cabin, and this textbook-tall, dark, and handsome pilot suddenly dressed in black-and-red outdoorsman checks and the tallest style of lace-up L.L. Bean boots, bolting the door against the snow and the cold then staggering in with an armload of the much-needed kindling with which he would feed the little pile of sparks until the entire room was Sunkist orange with light.

"Uh, rekindling. Uh ..." I looked past him to Psychology, as if I expected the correct title to fall to the floor in its effort to help. "Uh, let me get Janet."

It turned out that she and the pilot had met once before, on his last trip through. So she greeted him enthusiastically and then the volume got turned down as he must have been telling her about the rekindling need, after which she led him to Psychology. They spent a good half hour considering, flipping, blurb reading, flipping again before Janet settled him in the overstuffed green chair between Health/Diet/Exercise and Cooking, where he could be alone to study his options. OK, there's that bookseller's confidentiality. But nobody said anything about plugging your ears if somebody's revealing their trials aloud. Just as helpless as I felt decades ago in the confession line when one of my louder classmates was in the box admitting her impure thoughts to Father Skoniecki, I watched the register, as directed by Janet, but still could hear how this pilot was craving one more chance with his wife. The legal proceedings were all but signed and sealed. He was far past the need for anything on that top shelf, and rightfully should have been searching for *Mars and Venus Starting Over: A Practical Guide for Finding Love Again after a Painful Breakup; Divorce, or the Loss of a Loved One;* or *God's Design for Broken Lives: Rebuilding after Divorce.* But no, he was in the market for *The Busy Man's Guide to Rekindling the Glow.*

The pilot sat in the chair for so long I forgot about him, and was startled when I went to the magazines for a *Farmer's Almanac* and saw him there in his cinematic tanned lugubriousness, reading from another book with a heart on its cover. Soon he was at the counter paying for the book with the heart, and saying he'd come up with another idea. He was out the door and floating down the escalator and in the time it took for Janet to show me how to change the roll of receipt paper in the cash register, something I nodded along to but was sure that on my own I would botch up completely, the pilot made a return trip into the store, bearing a bag from Hannoush, one of the two—count-'em-two—full-service high-end jewelry stores that are among the first-floor tenants. He removed from the bag a small black velvet box, and unclicked the lid. Nesting inside was his idea of fuel for rekindling: a pair of quarter-size gold earrings, circular and curving like nautiluses.

"Think she'll like them." He said that rather than asked.

"She will," Janet assured him.

"Next time through, I'll let you know if she did." The pilot was smiling now, looking hopeful and buoyed and all those other light and bouncy things you are when you suddenly are of the mind that what you want just might happen. The belief that if you strike heavy karat-gold metal to a book with a heart on the cover, there's a good chance you might actually create a spark.

You could stand around and reflect on such Hallmarkian life moments, but there's work to do. It's the start of April. Which means it's way past time to get ready for Mother's Day, and late for Easter prep.

I roll the squeaky cart to Religion, which is opposite the children's area that makes up the far end of the store. Religion takes up three shelves, plus the top of the fourth and final set of shelves in that aisle. Below that begins the Native American section, titles for which are selected by Pat. At the bottom is a mishmash of spells, Wicca, tarot, palmistry, dream interpretation, and a full last shelf packed with Sydney Omar's annual guides for your particular astrological sign.

Bibles, Christian Q&A, kids' prayers by the pope, big thinky suppositions of what Jesus was like, I load all that onto the cart. In a nod to secularism, I visit Children's and look for anything with a rabbit or chick on the cover. I wheel it all to the tables that once held St. Patrick's Day, figure the green tablecloth will look springy so I leave it there, and I start to set up the books. Nearby, Flo is harvesting the St. Patrick's Day cards from the white wire card rack. There were maybe two dozen different cards available for that day. Easter might need an additional rack. Next to Flo is a huge rectangular box stuffed with holiday greetings and imprinted with the name *Renaissance,* which supplies most of the cards in the store.

Greeting cards are huge, and are the third in the trinity of the store's vital but small-profit items. Compared to newspapers and magazines, the 50 percent profit is sky-high. But remember, that's 50 percent of $1.50 or $1.95. Sometimes up to $3.75, but not often. What is often is the purchase of a fistful of cards all at once. I've seen people spend an hour looking, reading, comparing. Some aren't concerned about the message, as was the case with the trade school superintendent who bought one copy of every card bearing a feline image, didn't care whether the inside was congratulating you or soothing you. "I just like cats," he said.

I've seen a few people come in needing a sympathy card and showing up at the counter with half a dozen. No, I didn't ask—they explained freely that there hadn't been a mass tragedy. They just know that, sooner or later, there'll be reason to send another. Some people stock up for the year ahead, knowing they'll be mailing, say, eighteen birthday cards over the next twelve months, so on an afternoon in early January, they arrive to hunt down the perfect card for each recipient. And just as I am asked to weigh the merits of the many Emily Dickinson books we carry due to her family home, and family plot, being only a couple of towns away, I am asked my opinion of which humorous birthday card is funnier. Or what would be more fitting for a teen, for a new boyfriend, for a fifty-year-old who's not too thrilled about that milestone.

"What kind of card do you send to a young soldier who's being assigned to the Middle East?" an elderly woman asks me, as if we have such a category. All I could suggest was something cheery. Sunflowers were what she decided on, a photograph of a tall row of them all happy and proud against a wide and hopeful cerulean sky. Beneath the inside preprinted "You're in my thoughts!" the woman told me she wanted to write her own message, which she confided would be nothing more than "Good luck, Billy" and her name, because, as she noted, "What do you say at such a time?" I asked her, "How about 'Don't go,' " and she didn't respond, just handed me the $2.36 in exact change and walked away.

Your more everyday occasions are dealt with in the cards on three separate sets of shelves. There's a large display that runs the length of Travel, Travel Literature, Business, and Computers, and is almost solely for birthdays. At the near rounded end is a vertical renegade row of thank-you cards to be sent to those who've minded your home or your pet. The rest of both sides of the three-foot-by-fifteen-foot display are all to mark the day you were born.

The other card racks are a third of the size of that mother ship. One is where you go if you need to acknowledge other normally festive occasions: engagements, weddings, births, adoptions, new homes, new businesses, vacations, retirements. The second is for stickier situations. Care and Concern is the category on the paper headers behind stacks of flower-covered cards meant to let others know you were just thinking of them. That you want them to get better. And in case they don't, or didn't, you will visit the other side of this rack, most of which is populated by Sympathy. The artwork is of crosses and Stars of David and peace lilies and reflecting pools, the sentiments are simple wishes of peace and elaborate generic descriptions of what a remarkable presence your loved one was. There are cards bearing full poems and essays, too, including the old sympathy card chestnut "He Is Just Away," which, to me, makes it sound like, no, don't cry—Uncle Jerry's not really six feet under, he's just gone to Foxwoods for the weekend.

These racks are restocked by a card company representative who visits every two or three months. I met my first such person the day I was stacking the St. Patrick's Day cards into a box for return to their maker.

"Have you worked with cards before?" he asked.

"No."

"I didn't think so," he said, as he gently but definitely took the box away from me.

What I learned from that card rep: you don't pack cards one on top of the next. You line them up on their ends, as if they were books, the spine, as it were, facing up. I can tell you this because that is the information the card guy gave me in great detail until the phone rang and I all but knocked Flo off her computer stool as I ran to answer it.

The greeting cards we laypeople can and do handle on a regular basis are the blanks that fill a pair of tall, revolving four-sided racks located just after the stunning Easter display that now greets you as you enter the store. The contents of those racks come through the mail, from several New England photographers whose images of farm and ocean and cobblestoned street sell well. Also shipped in are Healthy Planet Productions cards, whose backsides state that they are "a socially and environmentally responsible company that is committed to issues of the environment and the protection of its animals and their habitat." Printed in soy-based ink on chlorine-free recycled paper are nature scenes and creature close-ups, the insides left blank on these too. Because many situations in life defy the themes of traditional cards, blanks allow you to choose an image to go with just the words you want to deliver. A soothing surf picture for a soul in turmoil, a jumping lemur when news is grand.

When the situation is, well, a little tougher to put into words, an astoundingly high number of Edwards' customers let Blue Mountain do that for them.

Blue Mountain Art's line of cards makes your sappiest high school love poem look like the stuff of a Pulitzer. I say this because I know. I am guilty of once having written sappy high school love poems, and of spending too much of that Papa Gino's college-era minimum wage on Blue Mountain products. In the late '70s, devotees knew Blue Mountain mainly as the work of Susan Polis Schutz and Stephen Schutz, who'd met at Princeton back in the '60s, moved to Colorado, and, when she wasn't freelance writing and he wasn't researching solar energy, printed posters of her poems and his artwork. According to the Blue Mountain Web site, they took their act on the road, selling the posters at shows. And, I quote here, "In response to incredible public demand, the couple's first book, *Come into the Mountains, Dear Friend,* was published in 1972. History was made in the process."

As were a line of cards, and boatloads of cash.

Printed on thick pastel paper adorned with watercolory mountains, flowers, or seascapes, Blue Mountain Art cards fold out to reveal often four or more pages of elaborately calligraphic, intensely passionate, and shamelessly over-the-top verse. If the "Happy Birthdays" and "Get Wells" of the traditional greeting-card categories are continent-broad in their focus, Blue Mountain Cards are electron microscopes of situation, emotion, conflict, and celebration.

In "A Message of Sympathy and Hope," the grieving recipient learns that "when somebody dies a cloud turns into an angel and flies up to tell God to put another flower on a pillow." That action is followed by a bird giving a message back to the world and singing "the silent prayer that makes the rain cry." According to this card, "People do disappear but they never really go away. The spirits up there put the sun to bed, wake up the grass and spin the earth in dizzy circles. Sometimes you can see them dancing in a cloud during the daytime when they're supposed to be sleeping." In the card's final line, these gone-but-not-gone folks are quoted thusly: "Don't miss me too much, the view is nice and I'm doing just fine."

I really should not pick on Blue Mountain, because this line of cards more than earns its keep. As a bookstore employee, I'm not supposed to judge choices of reading material, and neither should I go jabbing customers about their selections of greeting cards. I should squelch the "You're really buying this?" and take their $3.75 plus tax and give them a bag and a smile. Because people who buy Blue Mountain—especially people who buy Blue Mountain—have feelings. Scripty, swirly, Karo-syrupy feelings, maybe. But feelings nonetheless.

A year ago this month of April, I'd yet to know that I had cancer. I'd yet to get the first of what would become a humbling landslide of get well cards. I have to say that once they began to arrive, I did not check the manufacturer. I did not care if anybody, to quote the legendary ad slogan, cared enough to send the very best. What stayed with me was that they cared. Whether through spartan verse or overzealous prose, the point was that friends were trying to tell me they didn't know what else to do except to let me know that they were out there.

A month ago on this day, Janet had yet to phone my house. Three weeks after she did, look at me now. Getting to Edwards a couple of afternoons a week, in something that isn't pajamas or sweats. I might still wear them on the other five days of the week, but for these two afternoons, at least, I'm dressed and feeling as if there is somewhere I need to be.

Because Janet wants that feeling to be shared by customers, and because she now has somebody to take care of some of the details, she's talking about booking more events and making Edwards a happening place. Behind the counter, she opens a drawer and takes out a calendar. Points to stretches of blank spaces. Talks about packing the schedule, having a signing every week. And any other events that might be fun. Do I have any ideas? Anything I want to do?

I say, "I just might."

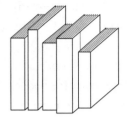

CHRIST IS RISEN.

So his display must come down.

It's not a big job. Items in the Easter display sold well, leaving little to return to the shelves. Hottest were the small $12.95 Bibles you see presidents carrying during Sunday morning going-to-church photo ops, and a much larger, more expensive one with roots just up the road, in North Hatfield.

That's the home of Barry Moser, the country's foremost master of wood engraving. Already well known through his illustration of such classics as *Alice in Wonderland, Frankenstein, Huckleberry Finn,* and *Moby-Dick,* in the fall of 1999 he became the first artist to illustrate the entire Christian Bible since 1865, when French painter and illustrator Paul-Gustave Doré tackled the job. Not that it was a race, but Moser actually surpassed Doré's accomplishment by making sure each book of the Bible had at least a single illustration. Using models who included waitstaff from local restaurants, he created a total of 230 engravings.

The original hand bound edition of 400 was priced at $10,000. Each of a separate run of fifty included handmade paper and original drawings, as well as a $30,000 price tag. Edwards carried the $65 trade edition. A bargain by any comparison.

Of the sixty we had stocked, no Mosers are left. The remaining items in the display, *Clifford's Big Red Easter* and the *Berenstain Bears' Easter,* get plowed aside for dear old Mom.

Hallmark ranks Mother's Day third among the major greeting-card holidays, with an estimated 136 million sold for last year's moms. If you're among those who see the occasion as nothing but a moneymaker for the industry, don't go blaming the likes of Blue Mountain. It was Boston author and reformer Julia Ward Howe who, in 1872, had the bright idea, but she planned it as a celebration of peace—an odd fact when you find out it was she who penned the words to "The Battle Hymn of the Republic." Anyhow, Julia found local interest for her holiday, but nothing further. Schoolteacher Anna Jarvis is the one credited for the modern Mother's Day celebration. Her original idea was to do something nice in honor of her late mother, another Anna, who'd often pointed out the lack of a holiday to celebrate females. You have to wonder if she were the type of Ma who might have hitched on a crabby, "Like me, for instance."

The younger Anna got the ball rolling in her city of

Philadelphia back in 1907, and seven years later President Woodrow Wilson officially proclaimed Mother's Day a national holiday. The quick commercialization disgusted its founder, who, in 1923, actually filed a lawsuit against the day, stating, "This is not what I intended. I wanted it to be a day of sentiment, not profit." Twenty-five years later, eighty-four, single, childless, and living in a nursing home that each May was papered with cards from every corner of the globe, Anna Jarvis told a reporter she regretted the whole idea.

By that time, largely due to efforts she'd made when she was still crazy about the holiday, more than forty countries were observing the occasion. Nobody ever counted how much offspring spent on their mothers before this holiday, but last year the average adult kid spent a little more than ninety-seven dollars on gifts for Mom. Flowers and candy are the biggies, as is jewelry, a meal out, maybe the well-intentioned mistake of an ergonomically correct toilet brush. They also buy books. So I get to work, harvesting from Parenting/Childhood/Education and, of course, from adjacent Psychology. I find inspiration from Religion, ideas from Hobbies, escapism from Fantasy and Gothic. I throw in books about investing, golfing, traveling alone, working out, bios of Eleanor Roosevelt and Sojourner Truth, collections of fiction by Latina women and African-American women and by women in general, and, with a nod to our own Janet, I find room for the first three in Janet Evanovich's numerical mystery series, favorites of my boss. I almost forget to make a visit to Cooking.

Onto the tables vacated by the biblical types I stack the new selection, and pull the card rack up close. The

Mother's Day cards have been up for a while. Flo had put them out with Easter, actually, because people like to be prepared. No matter who they are, I learn. Because I'm a daughter, all my life I have gone right to the From Daughter slots on the card racks. But when you're in the position of stocking said racks, you will find cards meant to be sent From Husband, From Sister, From Friend, From Boss, From Pet, and the generic From Someone Who Cares. I find a whole raft of Mother's Day cards meant to be sent by people whom the intended recipient probably never once dressed in embarrassingly ill-fitting handmades. I also note that the borders of the holiday have opened up in a very modern something-for-everybody way. There are Mother's Day cards for aunts, cousins, friends, mothers of friends. And more than a few cards aimed at those who came close to being maternal; the title over those slots is the (I hope) unintentionally angry-sounding Like a Mother.

I bump all these well-wishers against the other rack that Flo's filled. A smorgasbord of Graduation, First Communion, Confirmation, Bat Mitzvah, Bar Mitzvah. These are boldly congratulatory, softly blessed, printed with religious symbols and diplomas—lots of diplomas for these times in which even neonates have graduation ceremonies complete with caps and gowns. Many of these cards are designed in the definite shape of paper money or check, and it strikes me that not one of the cards for Mother's Day is made this way. None bear even a hint of a capacious currency pocket hidden inside. I have one of those floaty moments that occurs too often in my head, lifting me from the present moment to a very-soon future one in which I am creating something—in this case, a money card for mothers—that might just make me a few million bucks. As usually happens during these episodes, a bolt of reality zigzags down on me from above and cracks my perfect plan. The sad fact is, I'd just be killing untold millions of acres of forests for nothing. Because it never would occur to anyone to give Mom a few bucks. Wouldn't she really rather have that thing they show on TV for making onion blossoms?

Graduation books are extremely easy to find. Not that there are titles on the actual process of graduating, but there are loads for those being launched into the world. *What Color Is My Parachute?* is extremely popular. Year-round, a huge seller is Dr. Seuss's *Oh the Places You'll Go*. Sure, Doc was a local, but the book, despite its prelearning-disorder-awareness advice that things will go your way as long as you're "dexterous and deft. And NEVER mix up your right foot with your left" is perfect for any momentous occasion.

There's a gold mine of little gifts in those tiny three-inch-tall books usually located near a store's cash register, $4.95 impulse buys that can be hard to resist. As a shopper in a bookstore, you notice the tiny artichoke-shaped book and think how this would be perfect for Aunt Bertha. She loves artichokes and here is an artichoke-shaped book full of artichoke recipes and lore! As an author in a bookstore, you see the dozens of artichoke-shaped books full of artichoke recipes and lore flying out of the store, and when the stock is depleted you take orders for multiple copies of artichoke-shaped books full of artichoke recipes and lore, you place the orders for the artichoke-shaped books full of artichoke recipes and lore, one or two afternoons later you remove the stacks of artichoke-shaped books full of artichoke recipes and lore from the Ingram box, you ask Flo's help in assembling the front-of-store artichoke-shaped display in which the artichoke-shaped books will be the sole focus, and you as an author in a bookstore think: I gotta come up with a scam like this.

I should note that at least this one author in a bookstore is thinking that way. The artichoke book is something I just made up (but now that I have ...). An actual impulse-at-the-cash-register hit is anything with Bradley Trevor Greive's name on it. Starting with *The Blue Day Book,* published in 2000, which has sold close to two million copies. Greive is a thirty-four-year-old Tasmanian who tried the military and advertising, cartooning and painting, and then one day felt a little blue. In a 2001 interview posted on the Web site of Dymocks Booksellers, a Sydney staple since 1879, he explained, "I was sick, romantically dislocated, broke and generally feeling pretty lousy. To make matters worse I then went and watched a Kevin Costner film, which almost put me over the edge. Luckily as a man of letters, I was able to weigh up my feelings and options and choose an appropriate course of action. I chose to eat as many high cholesterol chicken burgers as possible. Then I started scribbling down some terrible poetry until I wrote the following line which, at the time, was exactly how I felt:

'The world turns grey and I grow tired.'

"I wrote this out several times, drew a tortoise sleeping on its back and then tried to imagine the world being completely made up of grey tones. Suddenly I realised that this was how dogs see the world all the time, and they didn't seem overly miserable at all. Then I started thinking about all those wonderful humorous black and white photo compilations from the old *Life* magazines of the 60's and 70's—and I started laughing. The book just developed from that moment."

Greive wrote additional simplistic text that could have landed him atop Blue Mountain (this is more than just a jab—the company holds competitions for new verses). But he skipped the soft-focus images and went right for the pigs. And the hippos and gorillas. Greive felt that his story of self-cheering worked best with animal photographs, spent weeks shuffling through his country's biggest archives, considered more than ten thousand images, and then settled on ninety. *Blue Day,* with its blue-toned cover shot of a staring frog, brought to light both dozens of pictures that had been sitting forgotten for years as well as a new direction for one rudderless young man. He's since published the pink baby monkey–adorned *Dear Mom Thank You for Everything* (first released in his homeland as *Dear Mum*, with lioness and cub embracing beneath that title) and *The Meaning of Life.* Another frog is on this front cover, but this one's green, as is the $9.95 Edwards and stores worldwide constantly take in exchange for yet another Greive title.

In 1997, Richard Carlson (a Ph.D.) set in place the first brick of an empire built on warning against unnecessary perspiration. His square little paperback *Don't Sweat the Small Stuff . . . and It's All Small Stuff: Simple Ways to Keep the Little Things from Taking Over Your Life* spawned a line of no-sweat titles, including a workbook. His wife, Kristine, even got into the act, with the 2001 *Don't Sweat the Small Stuff for Women: Simple and Practical Ways to Do What Matters Most and Find Time for You.*

"I want a gig like this," I tell Janet as, for the graduation display, I pluck more tiny tomes from the spinner near the counter, where *The Pocket Dalai Lama* and *What Cats Teach Us* and *Esquire's* 100 *Things a Man Should Know about Style* are stacked next to *The Art of War* and an advice guide for grandparents titled *Always Have Popsicles.*

"Excuse me?"

I once wrote a newspaper story about a bed-and-breakfast in my neighboring town of Ware whose owners, one weekend per month, handed the reins to people who were mulling over the idea of becoming innkeepers. The three days and two nights were a wake-up call to the majority, who'd viewed the job as nothing much more than redecorating in Laura Ashley, making a few beds, and knowing the directions to the local Museum of Old Musty Stuff Nobody Can Identify. I realize how lucky I am to work at Edwards, where I do little more than play, while Janet shoulders the hard parts—sometimes with great peril. Check out this recent e-mail, a response to my innocent, "How was Saturday?" "It would have been a steady noneventful day if I had not opened an inch-and-a-half checkmark-shaped wound on my forehead by misjudging the proximity of the plastic shelf sticking out behind the counter. I went to the emergency room and got seven stitches and came back to work. Yawn. All in a day at the bookstore."

Those days vary, as do the array of jobs each person

holds. Sometimes it's cashier, sometimes it's literary tour guide. Sometimes it's just collector of yet another story.

"Do you have *Business West?*" asks the lady on the phone.

I look over to the base of the *Union-News*'s big white plastic stand. I see a stack of the newspaper she wants, a locally produced newsmagazine dealing with well, business, out here in, well, the west. I give her the good news.

"We do."

"How much is it?"

"Two dollars."

"How can I get it?"

"Well, we're in Tower Square, at the top of the escalator—"

She cuts me off: "But I was just down there."

"Well, next time you're in—"

"I don't know when that will be. I live in Wilbraham." Despite Wilbraham being only maybe a dozen miles down the road, she says this like it's in another time zone.

"Well, do you know anyone who's coming into the city?"

"No."

"Then you could give us a credit card number for the payment and postage and we can send it—"

Again she rams in. "It's not that I don't trust you, but I don't."

What do you say to that? As I'm wondering, she asks, "I don't suppose you could look in there and cut out the article I want and mail it to me?"

I'm wildly sorting through categories of nuts to find

the proper bin in which her type would be located. Meanwhile, she's realized the same thing I have, and asks, "But then *you'd* have to buy it, wouldn't you?"

"Yes, I'd have to buy it, and cut it up, and send you the article you want."

"And you wouldn't do that?"

I move seamlessly to the next half hour's job: event planner. Because, did I mention? we're having a birthday party for Bob Dylan.

He'll be sixty on May twenty-fourth, and when Janet had asked me last month about ideas for new and different events, a party for Uncle Bob was one of them.

As was an art exhibit. Edwards is no gallery, but we do have some wall space, and I nepotistically invited my friend Susan to hang some of her paintings. Other than being my pal, she's second mother to my pup Leo, and an accomplished artist who's exhibited professionally as well as charitably, donating the use of a dozen paintings for the 2001 Farm Aid benefit calendar. And there are two other reasons for bringing in her and her work: a local cable-access program has begun a series titled "Paint New England with Susan Tilton Pecora," and Northern Lights Press has included one of Susan's pieces in *Splash 7,* its most recent collection of works by American watercolorists.

So on a Thursday night in mid-May, Susan is on the little stage in the corner of the Children's section, chatting away while standing at her easel as she paints cliff, lighthouse, and ocean. Then she flips on her hair dryer. It's her secret to pushing around the paint and thus creating all those gorgeous skies—"As seen in *Splash* 7," I shamelessly advertise above the noise of the Conair.

A week or so later, the same stage will become the site of the open microphone, a publicized portion of Bob's birthday that has resulted in phone calls from people who want to book their ten minutes in the spotlight. Bob wanna-bes, including a realtor, a mechanic, a college student, and a minister.

Next to me, Flo is receiving Dylan-related books. How to play Bob on the harmonica. On the guitar. Collections of his lyrics, for those who never took the language course. Coffee-table titles with page after page of how Bob looked long before he turned into Salvador Dalí.

I'm phoning newspapers and TV, seeking coverage of the big event at which there will be music, birthday cake, even a look-alike contest. I realize I'm getting a weird feeling from the whole process. Then I identify it: fun. I am having fun doing this. There is something about the work that is connecting me to the me of a year ago, the me I was before the diagnosis. That person wasn't within a day's plane ride of perfect, but I at least had an idea of who she was.

Janet, who's already somewhat nervous about how Bob's party is going to fly, overhears the mention of costumes. "You're telling people to dress as Bob?"

"Suzanne can do anything she wants," says Flo.

Case closed.

On the third afternoon I worked at the store, I was asking if I could move this shelf or change a sign or do something else I figured I shouldn't just undertake without permission. Flo's answer has become a running joke, one I enjoy repeating to Janet. "You don't have to ask if there's something you want to do," Flo told me. "You can do whatever you want!"

So the press release asked people to attend in costume—a Bob-like one or that of a Bob song character. I had planned to wear my twenty-three-year-old T-shirt from the Street Legal tour I'd caught at the Portland Civic Center during college and a wide-brimmed hat not unlike the one on the cover of *Desire*. I didn't know I'd also be wearing a neck brace.

Since ending the radiation treatments, in an effort to shake the feeling that I was now living in unfamiliar skin, I'd been making the most of my health insurance, regularly visiting a psychotherapist, a chiropractor, and an acupressurist.

"We're your SWAT team" is how acupressurist Blain put it one afternoon as his hands headed for my depleted kidney adrenals.

My visits to Blain were the most anticipated of any made to the team. They involved no cracking sounds, no probing neglected corners of the soul. Each was ninety minutes of receiving the bliss that comes from attention to the meridians I never even knew I had. The only sounds were the hypnotic wave action from the CD player, and me asking for my next appointment.

I was headed to another session of sought-after peace three days before Bob's birthday, driving along a wood-lined straightaway between Belchertown and Amherst at nine A.M., when the deer leaped from the forest. It was positioned squarely in front of my fender when I hit it. It then seemed to make a leap that was probably just momentum, then it vanished. Then I was slowing, pulling over, not sure what had happened other than I had just killed something huge and beautiful, and if I'd been feeling generally low before this, I was now officially subterranean.

I pulled over, as did the car in front of me and the one just after me. Shaking, I stepped out, looked toward the silent woods, down at the inverted V that was the hood of my car, crouched in the sand, and started to cry.

The woman from the first car asked if I was hurt. I said, "I had a nice life. And then I got cancer. And then I got confused. And then I got depressed. And now I killed a deer." She looked at me for a few seconds before asking cheerfully, "Are you the one who writes the books?"

Three days later, Bob Dylan's sixtieth birthday party was celebrated at Edwards Books. Where two hundred and fifty people jammed into the little store, where rows of folding chairs held an audience for the open mike to which one guy lugged an enormous electric keyboard, where a music dealer sold CDs next to the stacks of T-shirts I'd had printed with the cover of *Highway 61 Revisited*, where TV and newspaper reporters showed up to write and photograph and film the hoopla at which one man who'd driven all the way from Hartford paid homage by stapling headlines to the chest of his shirt. Maybe not the chest-stapled forty pounds of them Bob sang about in "Stuck inside of Mobile with the Memphis Blues Again," but who's counting when you're eating cake and grading the trivia contest sheets, dressed in your twenty-three-year-old T-shirt and big old hat and brand-new neck brace made festive with a cut-out of Bob's face, when you're someplace where you're actually having fun.

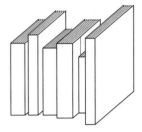

BEGINNING OF SUMMER. START OF THE RUSH
to read.

People appear at the counter, brows furrowed, frowning, rubbing heads over the big horrible problem of going
away on vacation tomorrow and having nothing at all to
read.

I ask the usual questions which I've learned jump-start
the hunting process: "What's the last book you liked?"
"Any favorite author? Genre?"

The answer is the usual: "I don't care. Just something
that isn't going to make me think."

I toy with the idea of creating a front-window display
titled BOOKS THAT WON'T MAKE YOU THINK,
and buying one of those foam head-shaped wig holders so
I can bore a wide hole from ear to ear. But I decide I don't
want to encourage that sort of existence. This is a book-

store, after all. The stock-in-trade is ideas, information. Stuff to fill that void between the ears. But some, ears or not, won't hear of it.

"Nothing complicated," one businessman tells me. "You know, something I'll just read and forget."

As a clerk in a bookstore, you hear that and you want to respond, "Right this way, I have just the thing." Because we do try to carry a variety of books. From Stephen Hawking to the Uncle John's Bathroom Reader series. But as an author in a bookstore, you hear that and you want to cringe. Because when you lead them to your opinion of a book they'll read that morning and forget by lunch, you hope that somewhere in some bookstore at the very same moment, a clerk is not leading a similar customer to one of your titles and is saying, as you are announcing now, "Pick any of these. Trust me. If you remember a single thing from this story, you can have your money back."

"Must be great to work in a bookstore," people have told me. "You can sell your own books all the time!"

Some of those people who say this know me and how I've spent much of the past decade—deep in shameless self-promotion. The bookstore job turned out to be a continuation of that. There you can—as I could and did and continue to—make certain that your books have the most advantageous positioning. In this one store, at least, no longer will I have to rely on friends or family or fans to relocate my books to prime locations. I can do that myself! Only one John Grisham left in the fancy cardboard display that's the first thing customers see as they enter the store? Sorry, John, I say, as the lone copy of *The Painted House* gets popped onto a shelf, and I fill the empty rectangles of the display with my own stories, flip around the sign on top that reads something like John Grisham's Seventy-second Consecutive Universal Megarecord–setting Best Seller! and on the white of its backside, take a Sharpie and write A Must-Read!

I've done that. More than a few times. But one thing I can't seem to do is the actual physical pointing out— "Hey, this is my book, why don't you take a look?" I might have a pile of them just inches away from you as you stand at the counter and ask for a good read, but I can't make my finger actually point. Closest I seem to come is when I'm leading somebody over to somebody else's books and she stops at the metal-and-glass shelving unit I've packed with copies of some of my valley's many, many, many local authors and poets. My books sit next to theirs, and if the customer does pick up one of mine, I'll say something like "I wrote that." The response is usually a weird look. And a "Really?" They peer at the book, like it's suddenly different. Right about then, I usually walk away.

I have passed customers with one of my books in hand and have said to them, "I heard that's quite good." Most have nodded, smiled. One informed me "Doesn't look it."

But none of that matters. Because I have Flo. Which is like having your agent, your publicist, and ten members of your most avidly supportive readers present at all times. In reply to the person looking for a good read, Flo is not averse to coming around to the other side of the counter, retrieving any or all of my titles, and announcing, "This is Suzanne Stempek Shea. She's a best-selling author and she's written all these books and she'll sign them for you." She usually messes up my name like that, but in her case it's cute. I stand there, only slightly embarrassed by the fuss. Sometimes the person is embarrassed, too, unsure if now he has an obligation to purchase. Flo is never embarrassed. She sees this as part of her job. Loyalty unbridled. After a signing, one out-of-town author was telling Janet about a hectic tour schedule and the demands by her publisher and what a chore success was. The second she left, Flo, who'd been at her computer with her back turned, ostensibly not listening, snapped to Janet, "She thinks she's a big shot. Suzanne's the real big shot."

What I am is an author in a bookstore. Where some think I don't need to be.

A woman places two of my novels on the counter. May I add that she did so without Flo's help. But there's still time for some PR on her part. Flo exclaims, "Oh! These are Suzanne's!"

"Huh?"

"Suzanne Stempek Shea. Right here. She wrote them."

"You wrote these?"

"I did."

"Then why are you working here?"

Because of the publicity given to the enormous sums paid to true big-shot authors, I find that many people think that most authors are up to their thesauri in multitudinous bucks.

"This is yours?" asked the man, when Flo disclosed that I was the author of the book he held. I replied, "Yes, we try to have all the authors in the store in case you'd like to meet them. Tom Clancy is over there in the corner." I pointed. The man craned his neck.

One afternoon, a woman who didn't know I was standing three feet away picked up one of my novels that just happened to be stacked next to the artichoke-type impulse-buy books and held it up to Pat, saying sadly, "I heard she was ill."

Pat was seated, arms crossed. She answered a simple "Yes."

"Do you know how she is?"

"I can ask," Pat told her, and with perfect deadpan she turned to me. "Suzanne, how are you?"

The woman gasped, "What are you doing here?!"

A local painter friend regularly is touted as one of the foremost floral watercolor painters in the country, and it was at a recent exhibit of some of those foremost works that Deborah Rubin told me she'd taken a job at an art supply store in nearby Amherst. It got her out of the house, was good pocket money, and she enjoyed being around merchandise about which she had extensive knowledge. We compared notes on having a little side job you love, and then found more common ground in the fact that many customers of that shop are shocked to find this very foremost painter dusting boxes of oil pastels. So too are Susan's new students, when they phone about signing up for the classes she leads; they express amazement that a woman with her own television show would need to do any other type of work.

Thing is, if we have to do something other than what we're meant to do creative-wise, isn't it wonderful that our other jobs can almost be like hobbies? I play at coining: Hobbs? Jobbies? Hork? Wobbies?

* * *

Whatever it's called, today it has me busy with Father's Day books and cards. Marveling at how much of the Mother's Day merchandise had sold. That had been my first major gifting holiday at the store and I had watched with great interest all that Flo and I had put out for perusing. I noticed some customers went right past it all, and because I'm nosey I wondered why. Did they not like their mothers? If so, what had happened? Did they not have a mother? Never? Or no longer? Had they simply already done their shopping? Or was it just that, like Brian Trelease, they came in to the store once, sometimes twice a day, and already could recite the contents of the displays?

With a change of gender, I had wondered the same when we were putting out the Father's Day cards. My father is dead. He was gone eight-and-a-half years at the time, yet I felt unexpected thwaps of jealousy when a customer brought to the counter a "With Love from Your Daughter" card to present, along with a John Adams biography in the more expensive hardcover version that she asked to have wrapped. There is no room on the counter for wrapping. I moved a pile of bills and a stack of special orders and a Poland Spring bottle and showed the woman her choice of paper—floral or manly stacks of dark-bound books. She chose the manly stacks, and as I snipped and taped, I peeked. Reading upside down had come in handy during my reporting years, and it did again as I decipher the woman's "I love you, Dad" above her signature. I wanted to tell her she was lucky and that I envied her and that she should repeat to her father the message she wrote whenever she sees him, because "I love you" is the last thing I ever said to my father even though I was just leaving after having a regular pizza on a regular Friday night with everything in the world still fine and dandy, as it would be for only a dozen more hours. But all I can manage to say to this customer is, "Do you need parking validation?"

My father wasn't big on books. The newspaper was his thing. Every night, and on Sunday the addition of one out of Boston. For decades he received the *Hockey News* in the mail and read it eagerly. Over the years, I gave him the usual Father's Day gifts of shirts, ties, garden tools. One year I stopped and asked myself what did he really, really like. The result was my most successful Father's Day present ever, and I didn't have to go farther than the corner store. Because, when it came to the material, all my father really wanted from this world was a bunch of scratch tickets and a pound of headcheese.

No organ meats at Edwards, so daughters shopping here have to settle for fatherly versions of Mother's Day gifts. Books on traditional male-type interests: sports of all kinds, wars of all consequence, barbecue methods for all types of grills, mysteries with blobs of blood embossed on their shiny black covers.

Kids are still graduating, so that merchandise remains out. A man approaches the counter with about ten graduation cards. I say wow and he says it's gonna cost him a fortune, both the stack of cards and the money that will have to be inserted. Another man buys just one. "Going to Rutgers for the ceremony," he tells me, and I sense no particular enthusiasm so, because Rutgers is probably five hours by car, I squint, and ask, "Do you have to?" He's taken aback. Exclaims insultedly, "She's my godchild!"

He'll probably drive from that to the wedding of his godson. It's that time of year, so I haul the squeaky cart over to Poetry/Reference/Drama, the oddly named section in which all things matrimonial are shelved. *The Mother of the Bride Book: Giving Your Daughter a Wonderful Wedding. Wedding Blessings. The Complete Book of Wedding Toasts. New and Improved Bridal Bargains (Over 400,000 Brides Served). The Bride's Book of Etiquette.* Because I like the title, I throw in *Things You Need to Be Told: A Handbook for Polite Behavior in a Tacky, Rude World.*

Thinking honeymoon, I visit Travel and choose a few guides for the brides. To me this section is like a candy store. Just a glimpse at the titles make me hungry to pack up and fly off. The covers, with the photographs of all those happy and spiritually uplifted travelers, make me instantly envious. Then there's all that information inside— city guides, maps, off-the-beaten path best-ofs . . . I pull down those guides by my two favorite travel publishers, Lonely Planet and Rough Guides, and hope the newlyweds will have a good time. Because I plan to.

A year ago this month of May, I was supposed to have finished writing a novel. But a year ago this month I was just beginning to find out that I had something wrong with me. I stuck the uncompleted manuscript in a drawer, ignored a deadline for the first time in my life, and immersed myself in the nonfiction of the real world. A year later, I still owe the publisher a book. So I'm back to work now on what I'd abandoned, and I'm off to do some of that work in Ireland.

My ticket is courtesy of my Visa card, on which every dollar spent counts toward one "mile," numbers that add up to eventual eligibility for an airline ticket. But it's not like you get a three-hundred-dollar ticket if you spend three hundred dollars. You have to eat through a couple of million dollars' worth of purchases before you even can get coach class to New Jersey. But the point is, if you'll be using a credit card anyhow, why not get a free trip every once in a while? Lots of people have these kinds of bonus credit cards, and I've seen a slew of them since starting at Edwards. Little corner logos that translate to a percentage being earned for college or automobile or hotel stay. Whenever a customer hands me the American Airlines AAdvantage card, I just have to ask where the bearer has traveled for free. We compare notes on destinations visited, then launch into the more important topic: creative methods for accruing extra miles. Every one of these card-carriers is an old hand at paying the tab for the dinner party of twenty-five, in exchange for the stack of cash being tossed in the center of the table. Did I know I could charge up to four thousand dollars for a down payment on a new car? And every single fee—including orphanage donation—involved in the adoption of a foreign baby? I'm not in the market for either, so I'll stick to my tortoise-like mile-earning pace from the usual sources: grocery store, phone company, gas station. Oh, and bookstore.

If you have even the smallest interest in the written

word, working in a bookstore can be like having the minutest nub of a sweet tooth and working in a bakery.

I almost did the latter, and I saw what it could do. My meat-wrapping job back in high school was almost a cookie-baking one. There were vacancies in both the butcher shop and the bakery the day a classmate and I were hired. It was a simple point of the finger by the manager: "You, there, you, there," and our fates were sealed. I was disappointed to be pointed toward the rump roasts, would have much preferred spending four hours each afternoon in the company of cakes. That's sort of how I see the bookstore. All you can eat—and with the great plus of sparing you what the cookie clerk eventually experienced: massive weight gain. Here the only loss could be your paycheck, the bucks earned today going right back into the money drawer. Even with that staff discount of 30 percent. Almost every title reminds you of someone's interest, hobby, problem, occasion. And if not someone else's, there's always yourself. Didn't you always want to plant a medicine-wheel garden, build a Web site, reread those classics that went right over your head in high school?

I didn't always want to tell fortunes, but I use my discount on what will be my companion for the Ireland trip: *The Secrets of Palm Reading,* a publication from thirty-year-old London-based Dorling Kindersley, whose dynamic graphics make any of their books instantly recognizable on the shelf. The book I owe my own publisher is about a palm reader so I'd been reading a book on the basics, but had come to feel I should upgrade to a more advanced text.

Even with the helpful drawings, I have a hard time

determining such basics as whether my fingers fall into the category of philosophic, psychic, mixed, spatulate, or elementary. So I shouldn't be surprised that in my rectangular (I think) palm I don't spy the good fortune about to happen on this very trip, and all because of my bookstore job.

On previous visits to Ireland, I'd poked my nose into any bookstore I found. The country's largest chain and main supplier of books, newspapers, and magazines is 185-year-old Eason, which has stayed in business because of learning early on to change along with the country.

"During the nineteenth century, the company was directly involved in the industrial and literary revolutions occurring throughout the country" reads *Eason & Son — A History,* by L. M. Cullen. "Our railway bookstalls became popular, but this depended on a growing literacy rate. More people could read and so written information became much more important to the country as a whole."

It's now important enough to keep twenty-nine stores in business in both the Republic and in Northern Ireland. Although the flagship on Dublin's commercial O'Connell Street has a Tattered Cover–like four floors and a café, most locations are utilitarian.

Ireland has plenty of independents bearing plenty of independent-intrinsic soul. Called "one of the most remarkable bookstores in the world" by the *Boston Globe,* Kennys Bookshop in Galway City doesn't disappoint the visitor who might have clipped that very travel story about this literary hybrid of bookstore/antique shop/art gallery/house of word worship.

For sixty-four years, Kennys has specialized in Irish-interest books and is the country's largest exporter of the out-of-print and the antiquarian. More than one hundred American universities use Kennys as their main source for Irish books, and the staff advises some impressive institutions, including our own Library of Congress. Then there's the store's marketing idea that, as an author in a bookstore, I wish I'd thought up.

Offered as a way to keep readers current on Irish-related books, the Kennys Book Parcels program takes your list of interests, and, to cover total and shipping, your credit card number, and every few months ships to you a selection handpicked from the store's more than 200,000 volumes. Doing the selecting is Des Kenny, son of bookstore matriarch Maureen Kenny, who cofounded the store with her late husband, Desmond Senior. More than 1,500 people in forty-five countries participate, so that's a lot of work for Des. Even so, he occasionally finds time to toss a note into one of the surprise packages.

I don't make it to an Eason this trip, or to Kennys. I bypass both and get myself to the country, to the upper bunk of a seven-pound-a-night hostel in a little village strung along a road that runs right to the ocean. I rest, I write, I have my tea and toast with a side of ocean view. I check out the community's modest business district, six or so pastel-colored buildings jammed together like they were all trying to fit into the same photo. With its two stories, a pale yellow skyscraper catches my eye. In front is a sandwich board that includes the word CRAFTS. I'm inside.

At the front of the store, a man with curly hair and little round glasses is stringing beads he's choosing from a

3-D palette in cups on the table before him. Finished pieces—earrings, necklaces, bracelets—hang from pins on the door and the walls, and they lead me to the far end of the room, where there are displays of pottery, soaps, mirrors, CDs, and a set of stocked bookshelves.

I watch the work of the jewelry guy, whose name is Jamie Storer and who is owner of this place, The Burren Treasures Craft Centre. We start to talk, about treasures and crafts and all such fun things, and soon he starts thanking me.

"For what?"

And he says, "Tidying."

He points to the shelf at which I'd been crouched.

What upon my initial glance had been a slanted jumble of cookbook, legend book, first-person-account-of-life-here-a-century-back book, coloring book of historical figures, guide to native flora, guide to native fauna, complete and total maps of the area has been made instantly neat. I've even weeded out his phone books, as well as a binder of what looked like personal stuff that had gotten mixed in with the items to be browsed by shoppers.

This is not work that I've gone around the world to do all my life. It was never my mission to fly off to faraway lands and alphabetically arrange the contents of souvenir shops. But since I've been at the bookstore, it might be. I mean, look—I didn't even know what I was doing. I try to explain. "It's sort of what I do for a job." I tell Jamie that, and then I tell him about the store. About the books I arrange and the signs I make and the things I try to do to make Edwards different each and every time I'm there because that is what a store should be.

Jamie agrees. Then asks if I'm looking for work.

"You're not serious."

"I am."

I had enough work already, back in my pack at the hostel, in the form of about a hundred pages I needed to whip into shape—not to mention triple in length. Whether it was truly serious or not, I decline the offer. I leave the shop that day without another job, but with an idea for another book.

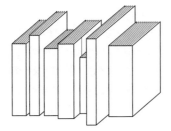

MY RETURN TO THE STORE AFTER THAT WEEK
away marked an important moment in Edwardian history:
The Birth of Stuff.

It started innocently enough. A simple Ziploc bag containing three or four dozen of The Burren Treasures Craft
Centre's beaded pieces. I hadn't wanted to leave the village
without a few souvenirs, and got to thinking it would be
fun to try to sell them in the bookstore. I start a lot of
things this way, thinking, It might be fun. . . . Sometimes
it is. Sometimes it isn't. Sometimes the idea takes on a life
of its own. Which was the case with stuff.

"These are great!" was Janet's response to the contents
of the Ziploc. And, "He wanted how much?!"

He wanted so little that we could sell a pair of earrings

for a mere nine dollars. Janet next said "Then let's get some more!"

I wonder if that's how it started over at Tatnuck, which, other than all that square footage devoted to regular books, the indoor restaurant, and the outdoor restaurant complete with fish pond, holds gift nooks dedicated to kitchen, to garden, to the Worcester souvenir, and what is almost a separate ministore just for New Agey crystal jewelry, tarot cards, meditation tapes, yoga apparatus, bath products, and scented candles.

Gloria Abramoff once gave me her take on the non-book merchandise: "If anybody told me when we were starting out that one day I'd be selling sarongs, I would've said they were crazy."

Thing is, she'd be crazy not to these days. Sarongs sell. Angel incense holders sell. Garden gargoyles sell. In a bookstore, books certainly sell. But on some days, it's stuff that really makes your numbers.

When I arrived at Edwards, the only nonbook or nonbook-on-tape items were a lumpy stack of fifteen-month-old T-shirts that had been printed for the city's celebration of the millennium. These and a shoved-off-to-the-side box of medallions, lapel pins, and key chains, all with that same millennium logo. You might've heard trumpet blasts when I cleared a table, dragged it to the pointy corner of the counter nearest the door traffic, strung the beaded jewelry over a few baskets, and stood back to hear, "What are these?" and "Where'd you get them?" and "Who made them?" and "They're how much?"—only that much?" Then, "Do you have a box for these?" and "Would you wrap this?" and, finally, "Are you going to be ordering more?"

We did. Jewelry, and more.

One of my favorite bookstores, for both unusual titles and unusual stuff, is Beyond Words, a twenty-six-year-old independent one block south of Bruce's Broadside Bookshop. Tools for inner development is the specialty there, with the stated goals of "Serving you, reinvesting in our community, and working towards a healthy, peaceful culture."

They forgot to add: "Offering some of the best stuff for miles."

I've often browsed their books on health of mind, body, and spirit—in fact, Beyond Words was the first bookstore I happened to be in following my diagnosis, and I remember finding the shelf labeled CANCER and asking out loud, "What am I doing here?" So I know my way around: through the journal and stationery alley to the left as you enter, straight on to the nook for the gorgeous chimes, and keep going for garden and path creatures, meditation tapes, incense, candles. I covet their line of "blessing bowls" onto which you can place flowers, crystals, treasures, and, according to the literature, "your desires, hopes, fears and blessings, as you place faith in the Universal Mother."

I place my faith in the Bookstore Mother, remembering that Flo says I can do whatever I want and that Janet will allow me the use of her business credit card, and I begin the ordering.

I'd like to carry a lot of locally produced items, so when

Janet and I talked about stocking a line of the phenome-
nally popular candles, I don't drive up Route 91 to con-
glomerate Yankee Candle, which Barry Moser probably
can sniff from his studio not too far away. Yankee is busy
enough running the forever crowded, sprawling retail
complex billed as the world's largest candle store, as well
as a year-round Christmas village with animatronic oom-
pah band, and a candle-lit gourmet restaurant. I opt to
shop in my home village, where several years ago a local
candle company opened in what previously had been a
divey neighborhood bar. From Candleberries I buy one
hundred dollars' worth of votives, which initially over-
power my car and then the store with their mix of individual lemon, vanilla, cranberry, and pine scents. Once
they're out of their boxes and into the air, the intensity
lessens, and they look fruit-store pretty, lined up by the
dozens on tables I've positioned just across the counter
from Janet's computer. As you walk toward your morning
papers, you pass between the counter and all that scented
wax. I already overhear enthusiastic comments, which are
identical to those that followed the arrival of the earrings.
And the sales are fast, as the candles are only a buck apiece.
People are delighted. Except for the woman who becomes
very upset to smell something other than paper when she
enters the store.

"I have allergies!" she announces, both to us and to the
occupants of buildings in adjacent blocks. "I can't shop in
a place that smells like this!"

I didn't think of that. Should have, though. During
my childhood shopping excursions with the family, it was
easy to find my father. If he came within yards of a de-

partment store perfume counter, he began sneezing, and could easily be tracked down to get that extra five bucks you needed. But when I got the idea to stock Candleberries, I was only thinking how easily candles would sell.

Which is the same thing I thought about the soap. Add to the store's mix of fragrance the lavender rosemary, cinnamon clove, lemongrass ginger, and sage fir emanating from the bars of Just Soap, which I was helpless to resist ordering after reading a *Union-News* story about how they are blended by a guy named Fred who sits on a stationary bicycle all afternoon, stirring the mixture by pedaling away and thus turning a giant attached spoon. Frederick Breeden loves biking and the environment and churns up these all-natural soaps in another place just up the road: the wonderfully named Florence. Janet and Christina swoop through a discount store one night and buy a couple of rectangular wire plant stands, and I use those for displaying the bars of soaps and the additional candles. The toys come complete with their own stand.

For the first time, I use a source that's south of Edwards. Down in Connecticut, a company called Melissa and Doug imports a wonderful line of wooden puzzles from the very Far East—namely China. Hard-as-rock wooden puzzles that last through generations of busy hands, they are shaped like animals, numbers, and letters. Melissa and Doug has toys, too—wooden tool kits with wooden tools inside, a wooden pizza with wooden rotary "slicer," shoes to lace, latches to figure out, and my two favorites: Jungle Bowling, a set of pins shaped like jungle creatures, and the fledgling percussionist's bangy-shaky

Band in a Box, which rightfully should include a bottle of Bayer for the parent audience.

Customers' interest grows, as does the amount taken in on register Key 9, the designation under which gifts and toys are totaled. And we know for sure that the items have become a regular part of the Edwardian scene when Title Man includes them on his rounds.

Every store has its regulars, and Title Man is one of ours. Maybe forty, slight of build, and incredibly well read if you're counting nothing more than the words on a book cover, Title Man walks through the store every few weeks and reads the titles. Slowly. Out loud.

He is not to be confused with Read-Aloud Lady, who occasionally can be found sitting on the steps in the Children's section, reading children's books aloud with all the necessary changes in voice and emotion. Title Man is a specialist. Moving along slowly, reading slowly: "Who ... Moved ... My ... Cheese ... An ... Amazing ... Way ... to ... Deal ... with ... Change ... in ... Your ... Work ... and ... in ... Your ... Life ... by ... Spencer ... Johnson ... Kenneth ... H. ... Blanchard ... House ... of ... Sand ... and ... Fog ... by ... Andre ... Du ... Dub ... Dubus ... the ... Third ..."

I am glad to learn that I am not the only one uncertain how to pronounce *Dubus*. And this makes me wonder if the famous and talented Andre, over there in his house at the sandy and foggy and eastern shore of the state, shares the feelings of this author, whose name is regularly Waring-blendered into Susan Stemek Shee-uh: readers can call me anything they want, as long as they buy my books.

House of Sand and Fog won the 1999 National Book
Award for Fiction and was Oprah's fortieth pick for her
original star-making book club. I've personally packed
more than a few carrier bags full of the twelve or fifteen
copies that have been ordered by book clubs around here.
So I have the feeling Andre might not spend too much
time worrying about sales figures. Do I worry? Well, I
don't lose sleep, but I do hope my books will sell. Since
my second contract I've been earning enough to keep me
from having to hold a conventional day job, but my hope
for some measure of literary success is about more than
money. I don't mean to sound like a starry-eyed heroine
from over in the Gothic section, but the main reason I
want a book to do well is so I can write another. Because
that's how it goes. You can have the gift of the writing
gods, but if nobody buys your book, there'll be a big fat
zero on the accounting sheet, and it's going to be next to
impossible to line up another contract. And while I write
for writing's sake, there is something very cool about getting to sit here, as I am now, on my patio on an August afternoon, in shorts and tie-dye, dog lying on my bare feet,
breeze floating through, butterflies and birds commuting
past, quiet—and I'm here telling stories. Sure, some days
it can be like work, but most of the time it's just fun.

So, for the sake of all that, I indeed hope the books do
well. And right now I have a whole new title to root for.
On this sparkling afternoon, over at the bookstore, the
UPS man has rolled in a cartload of my new novel.

When your new book is printed, your publisher sends
a few copies to your home. You get your first look then,
and, if you're like me, you don't stop looking for maybe

the rest of the day. Ten years ago, when I received the hard-cover of my first novel in the Saturday morning mail, I drove around until dark, barging in on friends to show it off, bothering relatives, pulling over to the side of the road and waving it at my cousin as he drove his lawn tractor. I don't have kids so I'm not sure, but maybe that's what you do with them too, just after you get one. Drive around and annoy people.

When *Around Again* arrived in the mail, my reaction was different. A fourth book! I'd been so amazed to pull off even a second one that on the night of the initial read-ing I took a photograph of the audience, pretty certain—simply because how many times do you get a book published—I wouldn't experience such a night again. But here in my mailbox was my fourth! Written during what had been an enjoyable stretch of time for me and then edited during my previous summer of dread and freaking out and a too-long wait for diagnosis and surgery. I'd edit a page and then have another stare out of the window or another flip through the how-fortunately-for-me-newly-revised *Dr. Susan Love's Breast Book*. The project crawled along. But I got it done, and proof positive was now in the padded mailer in my hands. Next step: taking it on the road.

But not before completing one more task at the book-store. I collect the histories and biographies and the Philadelphia and Washington travel guides that were the Independence Day display, and, in their place, I put up me me me. From my horse pal Maytaz, I've borrowed a saddle and bridle, which I place on a glass table in the front window. Beneath them, I set a pair of riding boots

I bought in Galway two summers before, not far from Kennys, at what a sidewalk sign billed as a MASSIVE SADDLERY SALE and where, because I liked the wording, I stopped initially just to take a picture. On and around the saddle and bridle and above those boots, I stack dozens of *Around Agains*.

I should back up and explain that the novel is about a woman who returns to the farm where she spent her childhood summers, and that the farm was long known for the pony ring on which several generations of kids have ridden. The publisher has sent Edwards an enormous enlargement of the cover, which is a lovely fuzzy illustration of an orangey barn at the top of a yellowey green field. I position the cover in back of the saddle and walk outside, which is really inside because I'm still in Tower Square, but I'm outside the store, on the other side of the glass, and from there I think the display looks pretty good.

This month last year, I actually thought ahead to this month this year, and at the time could not picture having the interest or energy for a book tour. I'm certain that if I'd also checked those resources at the beginning of March, I would have felt the same. But since the middle of March, it's as if I've been in training for these next couple of weeks. I've been hanging around a bookstore, which is the bulk of a book tour, but I've also been hanging around in the world. I slid off the little chair I'd curled into, realized that I actually could get through an afternoon without a nap, stopped jumping into spaces below the counter when Janet wants to introduce me to someone, and can converse with Mrs. Sharpe, who has become a major consumer of Just Soap's lavender rosemary. From the zero of hiding out at home to the sixty of being out on the road, I'm going now a decent speed of, say, thirty-seven. No danger of whiplash as I begin the tour.

As usual, it begins at Bruce's. My start for each of the three previous books. Bruce was a strong supporter of local authors, and we were introduced a dozen years back by one of them—Elinor Lipman, bestselling best friend to so many new authors—who, a few months before, out of the blue, had become my friend and my fairy bookmother, steering my first story into the hands of an agent and an editor. At the time of our first conversation, I was still finishing that manuscript, but Bruce didn't care. Just told me that when it was published, I could do my first reading at his store.

He didn't ask to see my book, didn't care who my publisher was. I mention these points because in the decade since that first reading I have met a few bookstore event coordinators who want to thoroughly research you before even putting you on a "don't-call-us-we'll-call-you" list. Bruce only needed to know that you had a story to tell, which made him especially wonderful to those writers just starting out. So many first-time authors' first readings have been scheduled at the Broadside so many times that Bruce had to consult the wall calendar on the column between the pair of registers and flip the pages to determine a date. Which is what he had done for me almost a year before, when I'd come into his store and, when he'd asked me why I hadn't been around lately, told him I had cancer. That's when he told me he did too.

There in the middle of the Broadside, at the exact opening in the counter where the podium is set up for readings, Bruce and I hugged. There was another bookstore box of Kleenex, questions about prognoses. I told him mine was good. He told me his wasn't. Before I left that day, Bruce asked me when my next book would be published. I told him it would be in a year: "Next July." He flipped the calendar to its last page and made that note. Suzanne—July.

Early the next July, I stood in that same gap in the counter to read from *Around Again*. As had been the sweet case at my other first readings, the Broadside was packed with family and friends. But one member was missing. Bruce, who usually stood a few feet behind me as I read, had died only a few weeks earlier. I told the crowd how at most stores, event coordinators, store managers, or shop owners expect to see me strolling in, pen in hand, no earlier than ten or fifteen minutes before the event is to begin. Bruce knew better because, before what was the first book reading I'd ever done, I'd asked him, "Do you have a loading dock?" I arrived about an hour before the event was to begin because, as I'd warned Bruce, mine would be a little different from the traditional wine-and-cheese soiree. Upon learning that Gallo and Monterey Jack was what you'd be served at most readings, my mother had called in the heavy artillery. With my honorary *Babci*, Alice Pilch, leading the pack, women in the four villages of Palmer and beyond soon were pinching their fingers to the bone as they made dozens and dozens of *pierogi* to be served in the bookstore. As my mother saw it, I was writing about people who were eating these things. The least I could do was serve a few.

So that's why on a balmy evening in late May 1994, Bruce was on his backdoor loading dock, reaching down to accept steam cookers, cans of Sterno, stacks of paper plates and napkins, and, most important, the insulated containers bearing the *pierogi*. He carried away napkins, cups, loaves of still-warm rye bread, red tablecloths, and department store boxes lined with Reynolds Wrap that held freshly fried and sugar-dusted *chrust* for dessert. There were vases of flowers from the backyard garden, the blossoms spring-vibrant and promising. All these Bruce reached down for as I handed them up from the car. He was chuckling at the number and nature of the containers. He was not saying he was too busy for all this or where were we going to put all this stuff. He was just being welcoming and helpful and asking me what else he could bring inside.

Bruce didn't know, but in that first half hour, he'd already also brought into his store my deep admiration for him and for his heart, both of which he opened wide enough to embrace new writers like me.

And I, three books later, did what one year earlier he'd put me on the calendar to do. I read from my new book.

The next morning it was off to Chicago, a place I always enjoy. It's been on each of my tours because it's a big reading city and because it is home to an enormous population of Polish-Americans (the claim is "more Poles in Chicago than in Warsaw"). In 1994 it also was the site of my first experience with a literary escort, and Don Lynch provided the perfect introduction. Funny, knowledgeable, adept at the wheel, great with the story, and very tolerant of hicks (his was the first cell phone I ever spoke on, and I had my picture taken with it to mark the occasion), he either drove me on my subsequent visits or simply showed up at a reading as simply an enthusiastic audience member. On one tour, he ferried me to Milwaukee on the spur of the moment after hearing me mention at a reading that I was about to board a train for the one-hour trip north.

The *Around Again* visit to Chicago found me going around again in the car of Bill-without-the-Ph.D. for that personal best of twenty-two drop-in signings in a day— no—in twelve or so hours. One stop was the wonderfully named Women & Children First, one of the largest feminist bookstores in the country. Located in a diverse North Side Chicago neighborhood, the twenty-five-year-old store stocks more than thirty thousand books about women and by women, including this woman, who read there several years back and who coveted almost every one of the politically and culturally challenging T-shirts lining the walls.

I did have an actual reading the next day, at Barbara's Bookstore in the suburb of Oak Park. Barbara's is a ten-location chain, the newest being a 2,400-square-foot store-within-a-store in the downtown Chicago Marshall Field's, the nation's second-largest department store, and an 8,000-square-foot store (with adjacent coffee and wine service farmed out to another company) on the Chicago campus of the University of Illinois.

On a tour several years before, I had stopped by Barbara's North Wells Street location during a reading by Marianne Faithfull, who was promoting her biography. Flanked by a cadre of assistants, she read two or three paragraphs and then quickly signed books for those in the packed house who had been given numbered cards telling them their place in line. My event would be a little more leisurely. I entered only with Bill, read and generally jabbered on for probably a bit too long, fielded questions from the audience of maybe twenty that included a couple of people who came as favors to mutual friends, and signed to those in a loosely assembled line who were free to linger as long as they pleased.

The Oak Park location doesn't have a kitchen, but I was offered a beverage, one of the staff kindnesses that included a pre-event rest in the back office, fresh flowers on the reading table, and a request for my autograph on a former-hairstyle publicity photo the store planned to hang. Like the Brookline Booksmith, Barbara's store allows dogs to browse too. In my experience that's a sign you're in a fine establishment, and a reason that, if only in the interest of installing that good-karma blessing, my own pup, Tiny, spent a few afternoons of her infancy sleeping behind the Edwards counter.

This was my second visit to Barbara's Oak Park store, which I hold particularly good memories of because my last time through was a tour I'd assembled on my own. I didn't have a new book out, and therefore no publicity funded by the publisher, but I didn't want to miss an October on the road. It's a hot month for my books due to its designation as Polish Heritage Month, and when I phoned Barbara's, they did a very Brucean thing: invited me to read, no questions asked.

I add a new cool memory from this most recent night there. A woman in the audience told me that she'd made an art piece based on a quotation from my third novel, the artist's story in *Lily of the Valley*. A few minutes after the store closed, Bill whisked me to a nearby gallery, which staff unlocked just so I could see my words as they appeared after passing through a reader's mind and imagination.

The next morning, I'm in the front seat of a friend's car, getting a free ride to Milwaukee. Jane Ungari, an English professor who has hosted me for readings at Robert Morris College in downtown Chicago, had been at Barbara's the night before and had told me she would be driving north to see her parents in the morning. So after a morning walk along the lake and yoga on the beach, I headed down Michigan Avenue for a sack of this amazing caramel corn from a shop that not at all subtly wafts the aroma of butter out the front door, and met Jane at my hotel. She was summery, car packed for a vacation, had lots to tell me. I was glad because I was in communications shock. I might not have started this tour at zero, but even from the Edwards-induced leg up on getting back to the world, I still was reeling from the amount of talking I'd had to do in a few short days. In Jane's car, I watched the souvenir cheese shops pass and the corn bag grow empty, until I was in Milwaukee, installed at the Pfister Hotel with its grand lobby and wide hallways right out of *The Shining,* awaiting Deborah Unger, whose surname sounds like Jane's, and who, over several visits with her as my literary escort, has become as much of a friend.

Deborah and I had a good visit that included touring a nearby street fair where she bought me my first toe ring and then treated me to a nighttime visit to a bar high atop the city lights. In between was what is considered the "work." Out in Franklin, I spoke at the newly constructed Polish Center of Wisconsin. Representatives of many local Polish-American groups to which I've read over the years attended, as did just plain readers. The room was packed, there were not enough chairs, and from the evening I took a valuable lesson: it does not hurt to turn a reading into a party. This was a fund-raiser for the center, and spirits were high. Music played as people tucked into the buffet of traditional Polish food, browsed the table of books, did lots of holiday shopping five months ahead of schedule. The festive air was like that of a *poprawiny*, the two-day party that follows a traditional Polish wedding. I have zero relatives in Milwaukee, so I wasn't expecting to see anyone. But that's how it happens. Calling me over were Wally and Dorothy Wisniewski, who came out of the blue years ago when I first began doing book tours. Back then, when I went to Milwaukee, I read at Audubon Court, a fantastic independent in the city's Brookfield suburb and the only store that ever held a staff pierogi-pinching contest in preparation for what they were to serve at my reading. Audubon since has closed. But Wally and Dorothy are still in the seats when I come to the area, as is Lou Jones, the brother-in-law of a western Massachusetts nun pal, Sister Catherine Leary, who connected us on my first trip to Milwaukee. Lou tells me he's now into yoga—but that's not the only news. My first visit to Milwaukee had been on the weekend of his daughter's First Communion. She's now a teenager.

The next night, with Audubon gone, I now read at another store in Brookfield, the local Harry W. Schwartz Bookshop, representatives of which had staffed the busy book table at the Polish Center. Now seventy-seven years old and five stores large, the Schwartz chain is the city's oldest and biggest independent. Son David Schwartz now runs the business for founder Dad, Harry, and has continued the tradition of hiring booksellers who know their merchandise and how to publicize. There are about forty people at my reading, and I even know two of them. Gregg and Michelle Pearson. Gregg's a former newspaper coworker, now writing for the *Milwaukee Journal* here, and both are faithful readers and reading attendees. On the way out, I receive a gift from the staff: a tin of little brass clips for marking your favorite page or line.

I say thanks, and then, "Where'd you order these from?"

Next stop is Minneapolis, where I know less than zero people. And the hotel experience doesn't help my contacts. I'm put in a suite on one of the many floors that has been carved from the great tower of a former grain mill on the banks of the Mississippi River. The accommodations are lovely, but rather spooky. Other than staff, I think I'm the only soul here with all those ghosts of all those sacks of flour.

I like that I can put my feet in the Mississippi, which

is easy to do because my digs are adjacent to a landmark on that river: St. Anthony Falls, the Mississippi River's only falls, and the site of the U.S. Army Corps of Engineers' Lower St. Anthony Falls Lock and Dam. I walk along the riverfront park, do my yoga on the riverbank until somebody creepy stares too long, and then get ready to go to Madison. I'm collected by a very friendly woman with a big van and tiny bottles of water and a basket of mints and an autograph book that she asks all her charges sign at some point in their journey with her. There are famous people in this book, you can tell, because lots of the signatures are illegible. On her page, Amy Tan has added little cartoons of the two dogs she carries around in handbags.

The reading is to be at the University Book Store in Hilldale, a suburb near Madison, home of the University of Wisconsin. The store is a branch, a compact version of the campus original, and stocks the requisite T-shirts and caps along with some textbooks and the many best sellers of the day. Plus that big stack of *Around Again*s and all my other books. An area is cleared for seating, and all the chairs are filled nicely. Again, maybe forty people. Probably not the same forty as the night before, but I can't be certain. I'm only sure of the fact that they're attending a reading in this place where I know not a soul. And then I see why: free food.

I have to thank my fellow Polish-Americans once again. They beat the drum very well, having arranged a side appearance by another author, local Joan B. Peterson, who, with Susie V. Medaris, wrote the handy *Eat Smart in Poland: How to Decipher the Menu, Know the Market Foods &*

Embark on a Tasting Adventure. Joan's prepared some baked goods. I read, I sign books, the audience eats smart, everybody leaves contented.

The next day, I am grateful that the very friendly literary escort woman has stocked her big van with little bottles of water. Because the closer we get to that day's venue, the thicker grows the traffic, and it looks like we might be stuck on the road for a long time. The woman has no idea why the traffic is so bad, but I'm wondering if there was some rush of pre-book-reading publicity—and that this is the result!

But I've been wrong before.

Among my fond memories of another deceased bookstore is seeing a crowd as I walked toward The First Edition, an independent once located in Chicopee's Fairfield Mall, original site of Edwards. The day I was to sign, people overflowed into the corridor of the mall and formed a line along the wall. When I entered, my heart began to jackhammer as I jumped to the conclusion that these people were here to buy my book—with my signature on it! Then I saw the sign:

Keno Is Here!

Electronic gambling had come to The First Edition on the same day as I.

You'd think I'd learn, but only a couple of weeks later I get suckered by another throng. Driving into the parking lot of the Enfield, Connecticut, Barnes & Noble on the night of my first reading there, I encounter bumper-bumping traffic. On the sidewalk in front of the B & N door, a fat First Edition–like line!

Silly heart kicks in again. I park in the only vacant

space, about a mile away, and wonder what it will be like to, Moses-like, part a crowd of my own readers in order to get into the store.

I never found out.

These folks weren't going into the bookstore. They were only lined up on its sidewalk. Because next door to the Barnes & Noble is an Olde Country Buffet that had recently caused many cases of food poisoning and, in a PR move that followed a visit by the Board of Health, had announced the apologetic gesture of free meals to everyone on this day, the same day as my signing.

So, here in Minnesota, I'm 90 percent well aware that it's a normal, very busy July Saturday in what the signs tell me is Historic Stillwater, so why shouldn't there be traffic? But I'm 10 percent stupidly wondering, What if this is for me?!

It isn't, a fact that is a bucket of ice water when the endless stream of cars in front of us begins to put on their right blinkers and roll across the Historic Stillwater Bridge, leaving us on Historic and now Traffic-Free Main Street, where we park and soon are informed by a passerby that those millions are headed for the Warped Tour, a twelve-hour day of very, very, very, very, very, very loud music.

It's very, very, very, very, very, very quiet inside The Valley Bookseller, where a toy train chugs along an elevated track beneath which a few shoppers pull books from shelves. I introduce myself to the woman behind the counter, and apologize for being late. She says it's OK, that she's still waiting for a few more people to arrive. She's hoping for a few more, at least. . . . I'm led to a little amphitheater-like area one level up, where three women are seated.

Early on in these pages I mentioned once reading to an assembled audience of two, so you know that this isn't my all-time low. But it's close. However, as was the case the night of the two women in the Shrewsbury Barnes & Noble, where I gained friend Sylvia, I now count among my pals Amy and Celeste, a pair of thirty-something friends who'd attended my reading due to ties with the Polish community. The third woman had wandered from the amphitheater at one point and didn't return, so I cut my presentation short. On a sunny July Saturday afternoon in Historic Downtown Stillwater the nice driver and Amy and Celeste and I adjourned to a nearby dessert place and ate fancy cakes at a sidewalk table and talked about life. Not exactly what the publisher had in mind for this event, but, I think, a lovely success.

Next up, Kentucky, another void as far as family and friends go. But that was the idea in sending me here. Forging new ground. Going boldly to states and cities where I've not read before.

Kentucky forging sounds good. I love horses and that's really all I know about the state: it has lots of horses. Another very nice escort, this one with a small car and a big sad story about her house recently burning down, drives me from the airport to the hotel in Lexington, en route passing miles of green pasture dotted with postcardish barns and gorgeous equinity. I'm installed in a hotel across from the television station on which I am to appear at five thirty the next morning. The escort arrives at five A.M. to walk me the several hundred feet to the station, where, for a long time that seems even longer in the dark in a parking lot at the back of a city building, no one answers the door.

You might wonder who watches TV at 5:30 A.M., but apparently somebody does. I have decent audiences at the readings I'm in this city to do, at Hawley-Cooke and Joseph-Beth, bookstores whose names you might feel tempted to swipe for your next characters.

I've told you about Joseph-Beth. Hawley-Cooke is the elder. Twenty-six years of age and with two locations. I am to do a straight signing, which is just as it sounds. No reading required. Sit, and sign. More very nice ladies, employees of Hawley-Cooke, seat me in a little conversation pit consisting of couches. The ladies have piled copies of my books around a laser-printed sign that reads Welcome Suzanne Strempek Shea. All the names are spelled correctly. I like these people already.

The store's sidewalk holds long tables piled with remainders, the term for books the publisher has decided to liquidate. Normally, a hardcover hangs around for a year and then a paperback version is printed. Enormous sellers might take years to get to paperback, as did *Tuesdays with Morey*, Mitch Albom's phenomenal best seller about his mentor. That was out for five years, earning five years of hardcover money, before being released in lower-priced softcover. That best-selling *Who Moved My Cheese* read by Title Man has been in hardcover since 1998 and shows no sign of going soft. But most authors receive "hard/soft" contracts that magically transform their tomes after a year in the world. And should those paperbacks not find the appropriate number of readers, bookstore tables like these outside Hawley-Cooke are the final resting place before they go to, well, we don't have to talk about that right now....

I have a radar for bargains and zoom right to remainder tables the same way I do to the clothing store sale racks that are tucked carefully at the back so that shoppers must pass—and perhaps be lured by—all regularly priced merchandise en route. Hawley-Cooke's tables aren't difficult to find, flanking the entrance as they are. I ask the very nice escort for a few minutes to check out the titles. It's my lucky day. I find a stack of *A New Path to the Waterfall*, finished by Raymond Carver shortly before his death in August 1988. Preface by Carver's longtime companion, the poet Tess Gallagher. Fifty poems that are the pushpins in the map of Carver's journey through his too-short too-hard so-brilliant existence. Was $12, now $1.98. I own the hardcover but I want to share this book. I take all eleven.

The escort with the small car and the big story about the house that recently burned takes me on to some drop-in signings. One store carries one copy of the book and I apply the signature; another doesn't have any, and I say to my escort, "Well, then we can go from here to the airport?" as it's the last day of the tour. The very nice escort with the small car and the big story about the house that recently burned says she just realized we're quite near the neighborhood that is hers but is not where she lives right now, not having the house, the house she asks if I want to see, and what am I going to say? No? I can see she needs to show me this house, which surfaces in most of her conversation with the regularity of a new crush. But the love here is sad. That's clearer than ever as she slows to the curb and pulls up to the front walk.

You think burned, and you think, well, nothing left. But there's a lot left to this house. A front, a side, white shingles gray, but a little paint would fix that.

"It doesn't look bad. Maybe someone can paint it for you," I tell her, trying to be kind, positive, something.

"You're not really looking." This is important to her.

So I scan. Take in the details of the place that was her home. Then I notice the top windows knocked out and the black-edged gashes in the roof. At the little added-on entryway, I now can see straight through the smashed-out door to where a back wall had been, now revealing just the green of trees at the far end of her yard.

"Oh."

I don't know the full extent of the damage, but it's clear there's a lot of work to be done if she's ever going to move back in and return to life as she wants it to be. Which is what she says she wants. She's just stuck, she tells me. Unsure of the first move.

We sit there in silence, looking at her damaged house, and, though it feels cruel to interrupt her meditation, I have to because it's time to go. "Uh, the airport?"

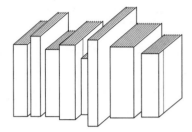

END OF THE SUMMER. START OF ANOTHER RUSH to read.

This one less leisurely than the last wave, in which vacationers were looking forward to seemingly endless hours in which they would do nothing but fall into stories.

Kids who were killing time at the neighborhood pool when they should have been knocking off *To Kill a Mockingbird* suddenly are flocking to the counter, anxiety searing their faces as they desperately thrust forth wrinkled copies of reading lists that last saw the light of day when they were shoved into a backpack three months earlier. Or they leave all that to Mom or Dad.

Because so many of Edwards' customers are downtown businesspeople, it is often the parents who sacrifice their lunch breaks in the pursuit of Junior's copy of *The Pearl* or *As You Like It* or some other title it seems is read by no one

146

other than those made to do so under penalty of flunking. If the school kids who come into the store this month look nervous (Do we have the book? If we do, do we think they will have enough time to complete the reading?), then the parents wear expressions of total disgust and resignation: "Kids—what do you expect?"

"I told him back in June to give me the list and I'd pick up the books.... But do they listen? How many of these can he honestly read in the last three days of vacation?"

I am reminded of the inspiration for the title of one of my all-time favorite books, Anne Lamott's *Bird by Bird*, subtitled "Some Instructions on Writing and Life" and definitely coming through on both counts. Back on a childhood Labor Day weekend, Anne watched her brother struggle to begin a writing project on birds that he should have started the very minute the last bell sounded the previous June.

As his son whipped himself into a state, the wise Mr. Lamott advised, "Just take it bird by bird," inspiring, if not the son, then definitely Anne and, through the grown-up Anne, countless others including me, who finds this piece of three-word advice applicable in most life situations—including the reading of *Wuthering Heights, The House on Mango Street,* and the *Oedipus* trilogy, all in the next seventy-two hours.

I offer the same wisdom to the kid who has requested all the above titles. And when the books are handed to him, he considers the thickness of their total pages and asks, "Do you guys have Cliff Notes?"

We certainly do have CliffsNotes, the proper name for

the classics-in-a-nutshell that have saved the necks of several generations of the not-so-studious, the tardy, the thick. Their covers, traffic-stopping black and yellow stripes, signal that help is right here! *Moby-Dick?* Guess what: it's about lots more than just a whale!

The guides bear basic information on the story's background as well as a synopsis of the plot, dissect all those complicated aspects of structure and characterization, plus provide author information, critical analyses, and an entire glossary of terms. For the most multiply layered titles, there are maps and even genealogies to help the story sink in. The series' founder, Nebraska native Cliff Hillegass, was big on books, and through paper routes and cow care in the early 1930s, he paid for his goal of a college education. While a graduate student studying geology and physics at his state's university, he repped for his college bookstore, and through his rounds met bookseller Jack Cole of Toronto, whose Cole's Notes study guides were published in Canada. "Couldn't America use their own version?" Jack once wondered to Cliff, who began CliffsNotes just before the beginning of the 1958 school year.

Sixteen Shakespeare books were the start of a company that now includes hundreds of titles in the categories of literature, test preparation, and quick review. Most are available for ordering or downloading on a new Web site.

When I arrived at Edwards, the CliffsNotes lived on the top plank of the set of shelves titled Computers, home to computer books, along with the Manhattan-phone-book-thick study guides for the GED and the LSAT and the ASVAB. These are study guides, too, but I felt they weren't directly related to CliffsNotes. So I grabbed an empty wire card rack, stationed it next to their unabridged brethren in the Classics section, and tucked each book of Notes into the individual pockets, getting an education— a fittingly brief one—about just what's been CliffsNoted.

The usual suspects: *Ulysses, Beowulf,* Plato's *Republic, Uncle Tom's Cabin, The Three Musketeers.* And some relatively contemporary titles, including *A Lesson before Dying, Joy Luck Club, Yellow Raft in Blue Water,* and *The Autobiography of Malcolm X,* which probably reduces the story of his thirty-nine years down to thirty-nine hours.

I made a CliffsNotes crack to one kid whose defense was, "They're a whole lot cheaper than the real book." He had a point. Where the "real" books on these summer reading lists might set you back from $5.95 to $14, Cliffs-Notes generally are $4.95. But there's a *Catch-22* to getting the Cliffs of *Catcher in the Rye:* you might have to use the real thing in class. Thrifty or simply nearly-broke kids lunge for the rack of Dover Books, which sells classics —the actual entire story—for only one or two bucks. *Little Women* for a tiny price, a *Heart of Darkness* that won't lighten your wallet, a copy of the *Odyssey* that won't mean a trip to the ATM.

I'll stop the bad jokes because, after all, Classics is a very serious section. It might hold titles like *A Doll's House,* but the stuff in here is lead-heavy with meaning and thought. I feel smarter just restocking. As I shelve books, I find titles I never heard of, never mind knew were classics. *The Custom of the Country,* by Edith Wharton, *Sanditon,* by Jane Austen, *The Secret Agent,* by Joseph Conrad.

I wonder what the selection process is for labeling

something a classic, and yell over to Janet at her computer:
"How does an author end up on these shelves?"

"There are exceptions, but usually they have to be
dead," she yells back.

So much for my idea of tucking my titles next to
Shakespeare.

I leave *Anna Karenina* and *Othello* and *Tess of the
d'Urbervilles* uninvaded. Go back to answering questions—
Do we have *War and Peace? Our Town? Ethan Frome?* That
book about the sailor?

"*Moby-Dick?*"

The kid squints. "No . . . it's uh . . . you know—about
the sailor."

"*Mutiny on the Bounty?*"

He makes an *uuugghh* kind of noise and surrenders.
Digs for the paper, from which he reads "Silas Mariner."

It's a grown-up this time, asking Janet for a book her
daughter needs, about a woman named "Mrs. Beau Vary."

Janet says, "Excuse me?" before she gets it, and leads
the mother over to the Classics and the shelf with the F's,
for Flaubert's *Madame Bovary*, which, in case it's new to
you, too, rhymes with *ovary*.

"Do you have *On the Road Again?*" It's a young woman,
college age. I'm thinking how it's nice to see a younger fan
of his as I type into the computer *Nelson, Willie.* She must
have caught him on the annual Farm Aid concert, or on
that credit card commercial. . . .

"I didn't know he had a book out," I say, just as the
computer tells me there is no such author. I type it in
again. "Let me try the title—*On the Road Again.* . . ."

"Yes. No. No. I'm sorry—It's just '*On the Road.*' "

Across the state, in a graveyard in Lowell, Kerouac has to be spinning.

Conversely, the annual search for classics draws some classic straight-A students. Both from public and private schools. Frequent shoppers include those enrolled at the nearby 215-student MacDuffie School, a private day and boarding school that includes foreign students with widely varying interests. A MacDuffie student from Vietnam paid for a copy of *Romeo and Juliet,* got as far as the door, then turned and beelined for languages, where she picked up that surprisingly popular book of Italian verbs and a general Chinese dictionary. Next, it was off to Cooking, where she browsed at length, ultimately choosing a large hardcover Irish cookbook. The city's afternoon buses bring additional students downtown after class. And when they have questions about books in the Young Adult Section, I send them to our young-at-heart adult, Flo. Though several generations removed from the YA section's intended audience, she loves the books written for this group, and often can be found stacking recommendations into the arms of young shoppers who, long before the movie version, were advised by Flo to read Louis Sachar's *Holes.*

Tim Kerrigan has read dozens of Flo suggestions from the YA section. He's also read as many titles recommended by Janet and found on the shelves of Hardcover New Titles and History/Political Science. Fourteen years old, he knocks off two or three books a week, and has been coming to the store all his life, a fringe benefit of being brought by his grandmother for a monthly haircut at Salon Caprisi one floor below.

A few summers ago, over two weeks of summer camp, he read the entire Bible (except for the Psalms). Usually, though, his taste runs toward history—especially World War II and the Revolutionary War. The Hardy Boys series started him off, he moved on to mysteries, then Star Wars. . . . He has nothing against libraries, but prefers purchasing books so he can read his favorites again and again. Tim supports his habit by dressing in red and white to work at summer fairs selling the family product, Millie's Pierogis, which are made over in Chicopee. The occasional gift certificate helps, too. And gets used quickly.

"Sometimes in the winter, when I can't go out, or when they cancel a day of school, I'll read ten books in a week."

And he doesn't mean CliffsNotes.

Christina doesn't, either, when she talks about the two or three titles she completes in a week.

Her favorites: *Angus, Thongs and Full-Frontal Snogging: Confessions of Georgia Nicholson,* by Louise Rennison. Michael Hoeye, starting with *Time Stops for No Mouse.* Eoin Colfer's *Artemis Foul.* "It's full of adventure!" she exclaims. "Every page you turn, something pops out at you! You never get a dull moment in those books."

She adds William Nicholson's The Wind on Fire trilogy of fantasies (sorry, only three stories in this one), gushing, "There are no words to describe how well he's written those books. And *The Giver* by Lois Lowry. "It just teaches you so much," she informs me before pausing, and then exclaiming, "I can't believe I forgot my favorite absolute favorite book ever: *The Alchemist* by Pablo Coelho. It's one of the most inspirational books you ever read about following your dreams."

Christina asks if she can quote her favorite line from that story, and when given the nod slowly recites, "Tell your heart that the fear of suffering is worse than suffering itself. And that no heart has ever suffered while going in search of its dreams."

These and other of Tim's and Christina's favorites are among those that sell well, and need to be regularly re-ordered. Many of the books in Young Adult are published by Scholastic Press, which is more than happy to be bringing you the Harry Potter series. With each new season of books, a Scholastic sales representative will visit the store to sit down with Janet and flip through the company's latest catalogs, while discussing new titles, paperback releases, reorders of top sellers. Like the literary escort, the publisher's sales rep is a creature you might never have heard of. But hang around the counter of a bookstore long enough and you'll run into a few. And if you're lucky, you might get to meet Rebecca Fitting of Random House. Smart, sweet, and hardworking, she's right at home in bookstores for more than a few reasons. At age eighteen, she took a Christmas-season job at the Borders near her Greater Albany home and got hooked on the book business. In the next four and a half years, she would relocate for Borders jobs in Peabody, Massachusetts, and Memphis before leaving the chain she says was getting "too big too fast. They had forty stores when I started working for them, and when I left there were over two hundred. I wasn't working in books by the end. I was working in retail."

A Memphis independent store called The Deliberate Literate was her next bookstore, and she worked there for a little more than a year before returning home due to a family illness, but that job would lead to another. The Deliberate Literate had the distinction of dealing only with Random House titles, a fact that led to her meeting many Random House reps, one of which would track her down a year later to tell her about an opening. Rebecca, now twenty-nine, worked in Random House's telephone sales department for a year, in Baltimore, before taking her current position in August 2000. Working from her home base in Albany, she serves a territory that includes all of Vermont, western Massachusetts and the Hudson Valley, and portions of New Hampshire. She drives to a client list of roughly thirty-five bookstores—all independents—in a silver Jeep Cherokee company car, twelve-year-old German-shepherd-Lab-mix Dennis often at her side. Random House catalogs are released for the spring, summer, and fall seasons, and Rebecca, one of the company's eight New England field representatives, makes visits to each store from three to six or more times a year. To take orders on the latest from her assigned Random House publishers—Bantam Dell, Broadway Doubleday, Ballantine, all Random House audio and large print, and the company's Value Line—she spends from ninety minutes to seven hours with a store owner or a buyer. ("I don't like to be rushed," she says, "and I don't like to rush anybody else"). If the meetings are on the shorter side, she doesn't run out the door when they're finished.

"I work in the store the rest of the day," Rebecca tells me.

"Like rep work?"

"No. Bookstore work."

"For pay."

"No. I just do it because I miss it. I shelve, wait on customers. It helps me in other ways—to see what people are asking for and to know how I can best help stores."

In my first year at Janet's, I will see Rebecca at the counter, talking with readers, making connections. Fitting (no pun) right in.

"I have kind of a unique territory," she tells me. "My most urban markets are Springfield and Albany. Quaint New England towns with the bookstore at the center. And the community revolving around it, most likely containing the most interesting people in the town. I'm guaranteed to meet those most interesting people."

At Edwards, she places Flo and Janet on that list.

"You guys know every person by name," she says. "As soon as someone walks in the door, there's a conversation. I think I'm even starting to recognize your customers!"

I'm not a Random House author, but some of my best friends are. So I cheer for their having Rebecca on their teams. I've met several of the folks who've repped my books, and at the top of that list is another late-great Bruce. This one Bruce Miller, who, several times in my travels, had just exited the store I was entering.

On a trip to Providence following the release of my first book, I introduced myself to a manager at the city's College Hill Bookstore and his reply was, "Your rep was just in here talking up your book. Bruce Miller. He just left."

I actually ran into Bruce a little later on that day, and when I thanked him he saw no reason for gratitude. Said it was what he did. And, I would come to learn, did very well, doing that talking-up at every turn, store personnel told me. Bruce also died of cancer. I hug his widow, Jackie, whenever I attend the annual convention of the New England Book Association, a.k.a. NEBA, where she pitches in behind the scenes. And I occasionally find her in my mailbox, in the form of a postcard describing the latest progress of her flower garden.

Add NEBA to the list of things I was clueless about, pre-publication. I now know there's an entire can of alphabet soup out there when it comes to booksellers' groups (most of which, by the way, know how to throw a convention). There's the Northern California Independent Booksellers Association, the Great Lakes Booksellers Association, the Mid-South Independent Booksellers Association, the Mountains and Plains Booksellers Association. It was at NEBA's 2002 convention that I was reminded yet again how reps from competing publishing houses also can be allies, mentioning you to readers and buyers even when you're not in their catalogs. As Karl Krueger of Penguin and Lynn Hildebrandt of Houghton Mifflin have done for me.

I met Karl at that 2002 NEBA convention in Providence. I'd just stopped at a display of Claire Cook's novel *Must Love Dogs,* had put on the brakes because of the title —and because of a basket of Claire's business cards, each of them bearing an actual dog biscuit.

"Suzanne Strempek Shea!" A well-dressed young man was extending his hand.

I hadn't known I was instantly recognizable, and coyly asked, "How do you know who I am?"

The well-dressed young man pointed to the name tag hanging from my neck. As I plummeted back to mortal earth, Karl told me he knew about my books. Read them. Enjoyed them. Gave them as gifts.

We're still in touch, and he's even visited one of my classes. I watched the candidates for MFAs in creative writing drool as he described his home decor: wall-to-wall books, and his job was to read, read, read, and then go into the world to talk about what he'd read.

I've yet to meet Lynn Hildebrandt, she of the legendary red hair and, something that's legendary to me, an affinity for my stories. But I know somebody who knows somebody who knows her, or works with her, or has something to do with her, and they say that Lynn, in what probably is another home with books on every spare surface, has been reading my books since her days of repping for Pocket Books, and now that she's moved to Houghton Mifflin, she continues to promote my novels as well as the two nonfiction books—counting this one—that are published by Houghton's distribution client, my own Beacon Press.

Two reps from two separate houses, rooting for me without necessarily being paid to!

I could go on about more good deeds, but it's the end of the summer and the beginning of another rush to read. Right now, right here, on this bright and steamy August day, there is not a clue that the world is about to change.

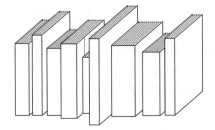

WE HAD LOTS PLANNED FOR THIS MONTH.

A real start to a calendar of readings.

That's a very healthy thing for a bookstore, getting people used to the idea that on a Thursday night or a Friday at noon they can come over to the store and meet an author, learn about a new book, have a new experience. For a store like ours, tucked away at the top of an escalator that, with no warning other than half an hour of little squeaking sounds, can choose to stop working, readings and signings are a way to attract new customers—including those who, upon entering, say, "I've been downtown five years and I never even knew you were here."

Very large lightbulbs appear over my head as I ponder the many directions to go. Having just completed the book tour, and still driving off some days for events in the area, I'm thick into the bookstore scene, chatting with owners or managers of both chain stores and tiny hole-in-the-wall independents. What's selling, who's buying, will electronic books ever catch on? Book people in general are good folk. They want to show you their store, how they've featured a pile of your books by the door and look at the posters they've made and check this out, here on the bookmarks—you're mentioned—and people have been calling to ask what time your reading starts. Sometimes, though, the manager wasn't told by the events coordinator that you were coming to the store, and there's a scramble to put out chairs and locate any of your books—do we have any at all? And what did you say your name was again? But usually, everything is set up, complete with podium containing iced Poland Springs and a Sharpie for signing, and you're welcomed with gratitude.

We want to follow that last example.

Now to figure out the details.

We've got the space, the chairs, the books. . . . Should we provide eats? I think of the readings I've done at Jeffery Amherst Bookshop, where co-owner Joy Gersten never fails to have her homemade baked goods on hand. She bakes for me, and for the big shots, too. There were cookies and squares aplenty at the megasigning at Jeffery Amherst's a few years back, when, in the same Saturday afternoon, visiting authors were Roddy Doyle and Doris Kearns Goodwin. Joy and husband Howard are busy enough with their sixty-one-year-old business, which includes a college store in a building out back, but they still find time to bake. Flo makes a mean chocolate cake—

baked up eight of them, Janet told me, for the midnight release party for the last Harry Potter. I could enlist her to add the touch of homebaked goods....

Whether or not we do desserts, should we do daytime events? I wonder because I'm just back from a noontime signing at White Birch Books in North Conway, New Hampshire. The store is a pretty little garden-fronted storybook building on the main road through that stunning mountain town. It's quite a change from its original setting in a local outlet mall, which is where then-future owner Donna Urey first spotted the store in 1992. She relocated it five years later, and hosts frequent events, including daytime talks during the busy tourist season. My reading was on a gorgeous weekday that found most of the town outside, enjoying the sun. The five people and one Maltese who weren't among them chose to come to White Birch Books and settle in for some culture.

So should we schedule both day and nighttime, just to cover all the bases? I think of the example set by Elliott Bay Book Company in Seattle, which averages ten events a week in its book-lined reading room, where I sat several years ago, one of maybe fifty or sixty people attending a reading at two P.M. on a weekday afternoon. It was my first visit to the store, which is located in another city's historic area (this one being Pioneer Square) and holds more than 150,000 titles. I just happened to see the notice for the reading about half an hour before. But several of those seated around me said they were regulars. Took time out of their day for a reading. I wanted to attend because the author hailed from my state and was a journalist, and his book was set in Ireland. His aloof presentation could have frozen nearby Elliott Bay, yet I didn't leave without being impressed, though it was by the fact that a store could hold ten events a week—at two in the afternoon, at five, and at seven-thirty at night—and, according to my seatmates, have packed houses each time.

Then there was the issue of souvenir stuff. Should we offer the audience their choice of Edwards stuff? The same week as White Birch I headed south to Dartmouth, Massachusetts, home of Baker Books, a 5,000-square-foot store with 25,000 titles that include an extensive collection of local authors and subjects. Next door is Remains to Be Seen, a shop containing countless remaindered books. At both, you'll find employees in the forest-green Baker Books shirts with the trademark READ symbol on the back. Think of the popular oval black-and-white foreign-country stickers plastered onto so many vehicles these days. Picture the word READ in the oval. That's what's on the stickers they give away, and on the shirts they sell. Edwards could make some sort of stickers. Edwards could have shirts. . . .

And mugs! I'm amassing an impressive collection of literary-themed models, the most recent being a Hawley-Cooke in the kind of formidable white china that could double as a murder weapon. The first mug of my book career was from the Brookline Booksmith, which, in 1998, held a local author party and, despite the fact that I live ninety miles away, was nice enough to include me. We authors were supposed to run the store for the night, shelving books and working in the gift shop. I wanted to operate the cash register (early training for Janet's), and so I got to stand up on the little raised check-out area and enter

ISBNs into the register and run Visas through the credit card machine. And before we left, we authors signed our names on a paper that would be given to a printer who applied them to a souvenir mug from which I still drink my tea. We could have one of those events! We could make up signature mugs! We could—

"Let's not get carried away." Janet motions to the remaining millennium merchandise.

So we start small.

I set up a few signings, don't bother with food for now, ditto for store souvenirs. I make a bookmark template on the computer, buy colored paper and a guillotine paper cutter at Staples, and Christina and I sit on the floor in the Children's section chopping up the lists of upcoming author visits. Nearby are big cups of french fries from Tower Grill, our afternoon treat. Desi Arnaz sings "Babalu" from the little stereo I've brought in because background tunes make the place more pleasant.

Mrs. Sharpe comes in for her paper, which means it's about three o'clock. A guy named Dave, too, but his choice of saved dailies is the *New York Post*. Kevin from the Department of Environmental Protection stops by, but thankfully not for an official visit, just an *Investor's Daily*. In to check whether Anthony Bourdain's *A Cook's Tour* by any chance arrived a month or two early is Rudi, owner of the legendary downtown restaurant known as The Fort because that's what was constructed at its site in 1660 to defend then-tiny Springfield. Fifteen years later, the town was burned to the ground by King Philip's Pocumtuc Indians. The fort survived that attack, but not its 1831 demolition, which in the grand scheme of things was a

milestone in the city's gastronomical history. Other customers whose names I haven't yet committed to memory:
The slight, quiet guy with the big square glasses who likes
newsmagazines; that big, happy guy who is very disappointed if *Jet* is sold out; Cynthia, always pleasant, picking up another best seller; fireman Stas getting the book
his wife, another Cynthia, had reserved. The thin older
woman who arrives on her payday to buy two or three more
mysteries. The young woman in cutting-edge fashion who
received the call that the latest of the Gothic novels her
mother collects has arrived. Mrs. Collins, a lovely retiree
who is always buying a gift for somebody, today in search
of a gift dictionary published by the Merriam-Webster
Company, which is headquartered right here in the city.
Bill's here, too. So now it must be just after five.

You can set your watch by Bill MacGregor, who works
at the bank across the street but who ends each day with
a chat at the store and a check if there's anything new
related to fly-fishing. He's a big castle of a guy, both in
height and spirit, a six-foot-seven-inch-tall example that
real men most certainly do eat quiche—and they even
make it (it's his specialty for any potluck). Having once
worked as a clerk at that original Booksmith, he's well
aware of the realities of running a small bookstore so he
doesn't find odd the sight of Christina and me on the floor
chopping up the homemade bookmarks to save the store
a little money in printing.

We're done with the task by six, when it's time to close
the doors and twist the little lock things that bolt them
into the floor. I've gotten the hang of closing the store,
which starts with closing those doors. I should preface that

with "starts with looking around the store for customers" because early on in learning the process, I once locked myself in with a kid who was lost in some fat volume over in the Computer section. So you check the store, you lock the door, you shut off Janet's computer, you hit the register's Z key and get a total of the day's activity, shut off that and the receipt printer, then you snap off Flo's computer, but you do so in a way that turns it back on to run a copy of the inventory onto a little square tape you place into its mouth. This way, should the system crash over-night, a fresh copy will be preserved. Go from there to the credit card machine, tap in the directions to make it print a long string of the day's sales and, via the same electronic box on which credit card sales are made, send that information to the bank to register the day's sales. Go back to the register and subtract the credit card total from the day's total, then subtract any checks you took in, and the remaining number should be the amount of cash in the drawer. With the help of God and calculator, the total on the paper and in the drawer will be the same.

The rest of the closing process is supersecret (and actually rather boring), so I'll skip those details and jump to the very nice part that Janet did the first night she taught me how to close. After you go out back to the big scary gray metal electrical box with all its many switches that you have to flip flip flip flip in order to shut off most of the lights for the night, you walk to the door between the back room and the Children's section and before shutting it for the night you say, "I love you, little bookstore." And then you can go home.

That's what I did on that day, September the tenth.

* * *

Back when she lived in Brooklyn, Janet spent 1980 to 1984 working in the World Trade Center. On the forty-ninth floor of the North Tower, as an office manager for an international importer/exporter of coal.

On September 11, 2001, after three or four customers said they'd heard something had happened at the World Trade Center, Janet walked over to the only place in the mall she knew there would be a TV—the now-defunct Batteries Included electronics store.

She stood in front of the screen, feeling, she recalls, "devastated and just hopelessly incapable of doing anything."

Her mind flashed to the fire drills in her tower. She knew exactly what it was like to stand at her floor's emergency exit. But in the best of conditions, when there was no smoke, no fire. Black humor was everywhere. People would say, "Well, we're fifty percenters. We're on the forty-ninth floor." If anything happened, they had a 50 percent chance of getting out.

"You realized in a tower that size there were risks," she tells me, "but you thought maybe a natural disaster—you didn't think about terrorism. They kept replaying the first tower. I immediately started counting breaks in the building. Anybody who worked there knew that if you looked at the outside, the design went up and down vertically in many silver bands, but there also were three stages that went around horizontally. I couldn't stop focusing on what floor it might have been on. I figured around the eighties because we were on the forty-ninth floor."

In her bookstore on the second floor of Tower Square on September 11, Janet received a stream of people looking not for books, but information. With radio reception poor in the store, she could give nothing other than a place for them to stand and compare scraps of news. That was the entire day. An effort to absorb the reality, to make the unreal real. Everyone who came into the store wanted to know what was the latest.

I was scheduled to work the following day. En route to the store, I stopped at newsstand after convenience store after drugstore after gas station, hoping to buy extra newspapers on this huge news day. It was half an hour before I found three in a Northampton gas station, where the clerk said what Janet would tell me another twenty minutes down Route 91: that people were buying the newspapers for their kids to keep.

They also were buying maps. No planes would fly for three days, and from the Marriott that was part of our complex and the adjacent Sheraton came travelers on business and for pleasure who needed to be somewhere, or who had airline tickets in several days but were hell-bent against boarding a plane.

To New Jersey they were headed. To Michigan. To Texas.

"You're driving to Texas?"

"Yes, ma'am. If we can find a car to rent."

We didn't have cars, but we did have some suggestions. We gave more people directions to AAA, where maps for far-flung destinations could be obtained. (Edwards has maps, but most of them are for New England and the Northeast.) In the home she made after leaving

New York, Janet stood in the shared shock, wondering if any of her old co-workers or acquaintances had been killed that day. And though she combed the reports and lists, in some instances she was not really certain for whom she was looking.

"I was struck when I heard about people who were in the towers working in maintenance, the elevator people," she told me. "The cleaning people, the people emptying the garbage, who made the whole place work. These are the people I might have walked by day in and day out."

That night, as I walk to the parking garage elevator, I see a version of those people. In this case, the maintenance man who always wears the crocheted skullcap and gives me a smile and wishes me "Peace!" He's wheeling his maintenance-man cart toward me, and, even though my elevator's arrived, I let the door close, so that when he passes I can hold out my hand and introduce myself, and we can find out each other's names.

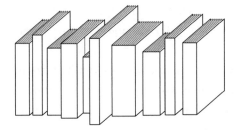

THE FIRST TO ARRIVE WERE BIG, HEAVY, HARD-
cover picture books.

A case full of them, each with the same awful cover and
the same type of awful photos on the pages inside.

"Ick," I said to Janet. "Who's going to buy these?"

I've mentioned Janet's black wardrobe. Well, after
9-11 she made a few exceptions, on several days wearing
what just a month ago would have looked like a fun go-
to-party shirt. Tan, with a soft repeating print of the words
New York, and images of its landmarks.

She was wearing it as a memorial the day *World Trade
Center: Tribute and Remembrance* happened to come in.

I cleared the front table of the back-to-school display.
Titles on writing, reading, encouraging creativity, a few
workbooks on math and science. I piled the picture books
on this same table, and by the time I wheeled the squeaky

cart back to the counter, someone had picked one up and was flipping the pages.

Next to be delivered was a paperback, smaller, also consisting of photographs, and half the price of the big hardcover. But the greater price of the larger book hadn't stopped sales. That first picture book was gone within a week. Janet reordered, and would go on to sell cases more, but without making a penny. All profits were going to a victims' fund. It was naive, but I preferred to think the sales were because people wanted to help, and, they may have reasoned, if they were going to buy a book on the subject, why not one that would help? I knew better, though. I know that tragedy sells. And that I'm not good around it—never was, still am not. When I was a senior in high school I was a finalist for a scholarship from the local Valley Press Club. I was thrilled to be invited to interview with the panel that was deciding who would get the money. I met with the members of the panel, in an office several floors above where Edwards is now. I talked about my photography and my writing, showed them samples of both. All went well until they asked me if I'd heard about the man in the plane in Boston. A week or so before, a small plane had crashed in Boston harbor. The next day's *Boston Globe* ran a front-page picture of the half-submerged plane on its way to being totally submerged. Plainly visible was the pilot, who would never make it out of the cockpit in time. Had I seen the photo? Yes. What would I have done if I were the editor—run the dramatic close-up, or a shot of it from farther away, or a later scene of crafts rushing in for the futile rescue? My answer was a well thought out "Uhhh ..." They had the front page right there on the table. You could see the man's face. I'm basically a mushball. I wasn't thinking that he and his crash were news. I was thinking he was somebody's father. And that's what I told those five or six people, who included a local television personality I saw each night on the TV news. I imagined how I would feel if were my father. I said: "I wouldn't run it. Think of the family—having to see him like that . . ."

How much my answer figured in my fate, I have no idea. But I didn't get the scholarship. I saw in the paper that it went to a Greek girl with a name fifty million miles long and a fat paragraph full of great academic accomplishments who probably went right on to head up the editorial board of the *Washington Post*. I went on to become a reporter, and over the years, of course, was assigned to cover death and tragedy and misery of the type that no family member wants to see on the front page—and that no mushball really wants to write about. I craved being sent to cover the dog parade, to review the old people's bell choir, to interview the Eagle Scout who's collecting donations of new underwear for the homeless. But a newspaper is a newspaper—with the emphasis on the *news* part of the word—and, though the man who grows Christmas trees is a nice story, it's not really news. People want to know what has happened in their world and some want to see a picture of a man who's sinking. Or who's falling through the air.

I had to keep remembering that judging has no place in a bookstore. At least not when the customer is within earshot. So I kept silent when somebody handed me yet another book with the numbers nine and eleven on the cover.

This was the first time I'd witnessed an "instant" book in action. I'd heard about them, and certainly had seen enough instant bios appear in bookstores before Elvis or Princess Di had even grown cold. But this was the first time I could see who actually buys these things. The answer? Everybody. And each person has his or her own reason.

For the kids, again, or for the grandkids, for their town library, for their own library, or yes, it was for themselves. "We who choose to ignore history are doomed to repeat it," one man reminded me as I handed him a pen to sign his credit card slip.

So, as you entered the store that month, to your left would be a table of 9-11 books. And anything else New York, which was what people were seeking. Existing books on New York—anything from the Travel section that contained pictures of the towers. We had to keep re-ordering a kid's book of New York City stickers, because among the adhesive photographs of the Statue of Liberty and the traffic cop and the Central Park buggy was an intact skyline. At the cash register we kept five or six copies of the suddenly popular *Twin Towers: The Life of New York City's World Trade Center,* Angus Kress Gillespie's history of the buildings' conception, which had been published in 1999. Kevin Zraly, whom the *New York Times* has called "the grandfather of wine-primer writers," had written several books on the World Trade Center's top-floor Windows on the World restaurant, and the release of his *Windows on the World Complete Wine Course* coincided with that of all the books about the towers' destruction. As a result, what was meant as an instructional for those mad for the grape became another collectible.

The day after the attacks, Pat had cut from the *Union-News* a large full-page full-color American flag, backed it with cardboard, and stood it on the table of books about our country and its history. Those got scooped up as well. I dragged another table next to it then squeaked the cart over to Religion, where wise coping advice from the wonderfully named Pema Chodron and Thich Naht Hanh is found. In Psychology, I loaded up on books about coping with troubled times, and from that section's bottom shelf, I chose books on grief and explaining death to kids.

Readers were asking for additional information. Bibles. The Koran. Anything about Islam in general. With this new wave of requests, I saw people trying to reach a different level of understanding. They might have bought the picture books, and they might have digested some of what had happened on that day. Now they sought information about who had done it, and why? What they believed. What their lives, their world were like. Karen Armstrong was the source for some of the religious and cultural answers. One of the most-respected commentators on religion, this former Catholic nun, who teaches at a London seminary for Reform Judaism, wrote two of our most frequently recommended books: *The Battle for God* and *Islam: A Short History,* both of which had been published the previous year. They were in hardcover at the time, and priced at $29.95 and $19.95, respectively, but people didn't blink, and we couldn't stock enough.

And we only stocked one book on Nostradamus when e-mails began to circulate that he had predicted the terrorist attacks—back in 1654. People didn't seem to know that the French astrologer had died in 1566. They were aware that he's considered a prophet, and that on the afternoon of September 11 their in-boxes had been stuffed with all these forwards about Nostradamus having foretold that "the third big war will begin when the big city is burning."

In rushed those who believed that if he said it, it must be true, and they're asking for a book containing the man's prophecies. Particularly the ones they were hearing about—which, by the way, turned out to be the work of a college student who'd written a series of them several years prior simply to illustrate how Nostradamus' cryptic verse can be so fluid you can draw from it anything you'd like. As did these customers, many of whom were the same who asked if any of the many newsmagazines now coming out with special 9-11 editions contained the picture that showed the face of Satan in the smoke of the burning towers.

Oddly, October is when a store should be thinking happy holiday. And not just Halloween, though I do want to feature some books related to that. But with the events of the previous month I will refrain from black crepe and ghosts. Pat has brought a Wicked Witch of the West doll that she dangles via fishing line over her side of the counter. Janet already is skipping ahead to December— and the following year. She hasn't yet ordered calendars, work that should have been done in the summer. Walk into a bookstore or an office supply store in October and you'll already find calendars for the new year. Not in this store—not yet, because there hasn't been the time. It's a pain-in-the-neck job that involves going through the catalog of the calendars that Ingram stocks. Dozens of pages containing hundreds of choices. As is the case with books and magazines, no interest or subject is left out.

"And it's like the books," Janet says. "You can have a billion titles on the same thing, say six magazines about the Maine coastline, and the one that someone wants is the one that is either sold out or you never heard of. Or that you don't carry."

So you try to order a little bit of most everything you can. Calendars with photos of animals, cars, nature scenes, foreign countries, sports, architecture, cartoon characters. New England is popular, I'm told, as is artwork by Claude Monet, Norman Rockwell, Winslow Homer, and anything mentioning Homer Simpson.

The calendar catalog has a big 2002 on the cover, a number that looks bookended, and also looks very far away from this month in which terror and grief are rung up constantly and you wish you had something different to sell.

Be careful what you wish for. In comes the UPS guy, and soon Bill O'Reilly is smiling from the top of a dump.

Dump is a bookstore term for those cardboard displays in which are displayed the newest, hottest books and the books of authors who happen to work in a bookstore. Except in cases like this, it is not a fitting term. Garbage goes in a dump, that's my point of reference. Here, books go in them. Usually good ones. But today, it's just those of so-called no-spin-meister Bill O'Reilly, whose photograph is being removed from a carton by Flo, queen of dump construction.

"You have to be an engineer to figure these out," she sighs, but despite the complaint she skillfully bends the black cardboard according to the page of instructions, inserts Tab A into Slot A and such, and soon there is a solid stand containing four deep rectangular holes into which we can dump *The No-Spin Zone: Confrontations with the Powerful and Famous in America.*

Dumps normally are set up out front so you can see them the second you walk through the doors. Because I know he'd prefer the right, I place Bill and his dump to the left of the entry. And just off to the side. So he doesn't get in the way of what for nearly six months now has been the store's biggest seller. No, not *Around Again*. Like everybody else in this town, I'm talking about *Ghost Soldiers*.

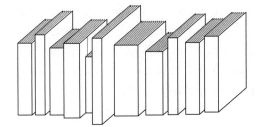

AS AN AUTHOR IN A BOOKSTORE, YOU FREQUENTLY covet.

You covet plot, you covet talent, you covet success. A big part of your day is devoted to this particular sin. You wish you'd thought of that concept, you wish your covers looked that mod, you wish you looked so confident and gorgeous in your author photo. New books are unpacked and you realize this is the one you've read all those stories about. So this is the preteen marvel who's the next big thing, that's the most recent hit by an icon.

What I coveted about *Ghost Soldiers* was the action at its dump.

Subtitled *The Forgotten Epic Story of World War II's Most Dramatic Mission* and written by *Outside* magazine writer Hampton Sides, it rests in the dump to the right of Bill O'Reilly's. There is a platoon of armed men on its cover.

And the man in the very middle of the lineup is the main reason why every single time I've been in the store since May, I've had to haul another six or eight copies over to the vacancies in that cardboard display.

His name is J. Frank Murphy. He was from Springfield. During World War II, he was part of a daring rescue twenty-five miles behind Japanese lines, on the Philippine Island of Luzon. When photographed, he was leading his fellow soldiers from the Filipino jungle, where they'd freed more than five hundred American POWs, most of whom were survivors of the Bataan Death March.

The book arrived at Edwards over the winter, in the advanced reading copy format that publishers send to booksellers and reviewers in the hope of the early buzz. Janet had handed it to Judge Kent Smith, a daily visitor whose counsel she often seeks for books dealing with history and political science. After all, the Judge has seen a lot of history, and knows well his poli-sci.

Following a legal career that included being the first "voluntary defender"—the forerunner of the modern-day public defender—and a lengthy private practice, he's in his thirty-first year as a judge, appointed in 1972 as an associate justice of the superior court and in 1981 as associate justice of the state court of appeals. He was retired on March 11, 1997, but only because he had reached seventy, the mandatory age for retirement. He was called back to the courthouse the very next day and has been full-time ever since.

He's an author himself, of two editions of the Massachusetts Criminal Practice and Procedure Volumes, which have been cited more than two hundred times as the authority by the U.S. Supreme Court, as well as by federal and state courts. So he all the more appreciates good reading, and his stellar memory can pinpoint the day twelve years ago that he walked into Edwards for the first time, accompanied by another regular, attorney Phil Callan. The Judge was delighted to spot a long-sought-after Gerald Seymour title, and right then he knew he'd found a second home. The bookstore is where you still can find him daily, checking in with Pat, greeting Flo (he's yet another grown man who calls her Mother) and checking what's new on the shelves. He lists his favorite authors as Alan Furst, Sebastian Faulks, and John Le Carré, and his top books of all time are Brian Moore's *The Statement* and Evelyn Waugh's *A Handful of Dust*. A rare combination of very friendly and very accomplished, the Judge loves to talk about writing and will chat up anyone in the store who's in need of recommendations.

Janet needed one that day back in the winter. "Let me know what you think," she said, handing him the advance reading copy of *Ghost Soldiers*.

In an instant he told her, "That's Frank Murphy."

Back in 1945, when the Judge was a seventeen-year-old freshman at Tufts University, he spotted that same photograph in *Life* magazine. He'd read every word of the accompanying story by war journalist Carl Mydans and was, as he puts it, "filled with pride. A guy from Springfield. Involved in something so heroic. How about that?"

One of five brothers who fought in the war, Murphy was a thirty-three-year-old lieutenant when he led thirty rangers toward the rear of the Cabanatuan prison camp in a difficult and slow advance past a guard tower and a pair of fortified pillboxes. The raid on the camp began with the signal from Murphy's gun.

Awarded the Silver Star, Murphy married, had two daughters, raised money for the Jimmy Fund, worked in politics, and founded a real estate and insurance company. He died in 1964, at age fifty-three, according to a *Springfield Morning Union* obituary headlined "J. Frank Murphy Dies in Sleep, Was War Hero."

In his early days as a lawyer, the Judge once shook Murphy's hand on the city's Main Street. He saw him another time, wearing a winter coat in the heat of summer, and shivering—an effect of malaria. The Judge wouldn't see the man again until he was handed *Ghost Soldiers* in what rep Rebecca Fitting calls "a kismet moment."

"I'm talking to Janet about the book, Janet shows it to him, the Judge says 'That's J. Frank Murphy.' It went from there. That kind of moment is so much fun!"

Within days, the Judge was urging Janet to read the book. Which is what she did several months later, when that first dump and that first few cartons of books arrived.

The Judge wasn't alone in word-of-mouth promotion. Sides had an entire cheering section behind the Edwards counter. Janet and Flo soon were chanting, "Read this, and if you don't love it, you can bring it back." There was the caution that it was not a cheery story—but this was war, after all. Almost daily, the Judge held a different kind of court, standing at the dump and orating about J. Frank Murphy and his connection to the city and about the masterful job Sides had done telling this story.

"That's J. Frank Murphy" would come from nowhere,

and you'd look up, and there'd be the Judge, sometimes with a colleague, often with an unknown browser. The strangers would listen but also would be looking at him with a "Who is this guy?" expression. Then their focus would fall to the cover of the book he was holding and gently tapping as he gave the facts of the rescue.

And another book would be sold.

The story of the Judge's realizing this was a city hero on the cover made it into the paper, sparking a tsunami of readers heading to the always half-empty dump. *Ghost Soldiers* swiftly flew onto the national best seller lists. And Janet was saying, "We've got to get him."

She meant Sides.

And she meant getting him for Symphony Hall.

Whether the author was at all musically gifted was beside the point. Janet wanted to add him to the slate for that year's Springfield Public Forum, a series of free talks by renowned experts on political, social, and economic issues. The sixty-eight years of speakers have included such household names as Richard M. Nixon, Leonard Bernstein, Arthur Schlesinger, Betty Friedan, Ralph Nader, Jeanne Kirkpatrick, Maya Angelou, Ken Burns, and Pete Hamill.

Janet's part in the series is to help brainstorm names and to bring to Symphony Hall from her store two blocks away a supply of books by the speakers for a signing at the end of each night. She donates a portion of the proceeds to help pay for speaker fees. She does a lot of good acts like that. Just a few weeks back she held the annual benefit reading she calls Open Books for Open Pantry, that latter open thing being a private agency that feeds, houses, and otherwise assists locals in need. Make a fuss over what she does in this regard, and Janet will not see the big deal. To her, it's just karmic common sense.

"If you want support as a local," she says, "you'd better give support. I can't possibly expect people to come into the store if I'm not going out there and showing solidarity with the community."

I was present the very afternoon of her foray into that solidarity, a decade ago, at a reading at the former Zone Art Center downtown, to which she brought books for a reading by Elinor Lipman and me.

"That was the very first time I took the store on the road," she says, telling me something I hadn't known. "Now I'm adamant about it. If you talk about reasons why we might have survived, one thing might be that we've been getting out there."

Now she wanted to get out there with and for *Ghost Soldiers*. Impassioned calls to publisher Random House were made and were effective in bringing Sides from his home in Santa Fe to a four-thousand-seat hall in Springfield. After speaking and reading, Sides took questions. That's when the audience—which included the Judge and Rebecca Fitting—learned living testaments to the story were in its midst. Two men rose to say they had been imprisoned in Cabanatuan, and were free and here tonight thanks to J. Frank Murphy and his troops. The applause could have been heard on Luzon.

"This is what a book can do," Janet told me.

I was thinking, This is what a bookstore can do.

* * *

Another thing a bookstore can do is rock.

As it did on another Thursday night this month, when we threw a birthday party for Neil Young.

Another party for another guy who wasn't going to attend. But we didn't care. Janet loves Neil Young. This is his birth month—he'd turned fifty-seven on the twelfth—and better late than never, we held a bash.

Publicity drew to the open mike fourteen plaid-shirted, guitar-bearing crazy Crazy Horse types whose personal fan clubs of friends, mothers, and wives cheered wildly.

Representing my town was Dominick Pecora, whose rendition of "Cortez the Killer" and "From Hank to Hendricks" were among the more daring picks of the night. As popular as "Don't Think Twice, It's All Right" had been on Uncle Bob's birthday, surfacing over and again on this night were "Old Man," "Needle and the Damage Done," "Down by the River."

Nobody complained about the repetition. It was music. It was celebration. After the events of the past few months, "After the Gold Rush" sung for the fourth time was not a world crisis. Neil's "Cinnamon Girl" shone gold as she floated from the strings of a CPA on the little elevated stage in the Children's section, across the store, out into the otherwise totally quiet of the mall at nighttime, delivering the message that somewhere on the second floor, there was life.

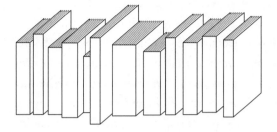

"C'MON. I'LL TAKE YOU TO THE DUNGEON."

Who knows what she's talking about, but the invitation is only from motherly Flo, so I consent.

She fishes a heavy set of keys from the drawer below the register and waves me toward the back room.

Pat is on the phone with Bob Anderson, a retiree and reader who calls every couple of days to add another title to his order. Bob used to work downtown and was a big customer then. He no longer visits the store, but his buying habits haven't changed. Every other week, Pat fills a carton with maybe ten or fifteen books—best-selling fiction, lots of new biographies, and many Gothic titles (his favorite)—and ships them to Bob's house. Right now, she's seated at the computer, checking the availability of the titles Bob is giving her.

On the second of the store's two lines, Janet is telling

a woman that the book she wants will not be out for another two months, and that she can put her name in now, and the instant it arrives, we'll give her a call.

"No, thanks," the caller says, "I'll just go online."

If you're not referring to a bookseller's own Web site, hearing a comment like that is like biting tinfoil. For so much of the population, online megastores are the way to shop. But their enormous inventories, their buying power (read: ability to charge lower prices), their sit-in-your-shorts-and-buy-for-grandma ease are a big reason for the demise of many small bricks-and-mortar businesses. All the more reason for traditional stores to stress the "let me find that for you" or "we don't have that, but wait here while I drive home and go get my copy and you can have that one" type of service. And it pays off. Edwards has customers who have vowed to never buy a word via the Internet. They tell us it's their vote against our extinction, and it's much appreciated. Others don't put it so mildly: "I could have gotten this online for thirty percent off, you know that? But I wanted to do business here."

You just reply with an "uh-huh" or "thanks" or "would you like parking validation?"

And to the woman who's going online, Janet says "OK," then hangs up and asks, "Can I help the next person?"

In the back room, Flo fishes around behind the door, and from beneath the layer of winter coats retrieves a couple of work shirts.

"Put this on," she instructs. "It's filthy down there."

As I pull on the shirt and follow Flo down the hall and

to the doors of a freight elevator, I picture our destination: a small cavelike place with walls of stone, damp and black except for the flickering oil torches on iron holders above the chains and skeletons hanging from the wall. Two floors down, there's the Tower Square belly—a wide tar avenue lined with a pair of loading docks. At the far end of the opposite dock, two blue trailer-truck-size trash compactors stand angled. Straight across from where we've emerged is the wide glass window that shows you the television monitors and various electronic boards of the building's security office.

We walk along the dock and Flo opens one of the many doors to the right. Through another just inside is a smaller hall, brightly lit and empty at this end. Along the wall at the far end is a row of empty tables, then banquet chairs sitting atop one another in a stack. Nearby, two guys in hotel uniforms hold a conversation.

Flo unlocks a door to the right and reaches inside, flipping on a regular modern electric light that illuminates nothing at all medieval—just a storage area.

While that fact disappoints, the contents thrill me. Dozens of square feet of shelving, wire display units, chairs, boxes . . . wonderful stuff that surely we can make some use of upstairs.

"Wow."

"It's just a room," is how Flo sees it. "Filled with stuff."

"It's a gold mine."

She laughs. "Years of stuff in here. The holiday decorations are in the back."

That's what we've come for. It's December, after all. Wrapped in drycleaner's plastic to keep them dust free are yards of fake garlands and puffy red bows with gold trim. In a box, Flo finds half a dozen decorative golden horns of the type you see fox-hunting people blowing on to alert the dogs. Flo mentions that they were bought a few years back at a postholiday 50 percent–off sale, and since forgotten.

"See? A gold mine," I repeat.

She takes those, plus a few hangers that hold long plastic-sheathed banners on which have been stitched the words JOY and NOEL. We unearth a bag of red-and-green wrapping paper, also bought at the end of some year.

There are several cartons of boxed greeting cards— both classy nature-photo sunlit snow-covered meadow types, and cartoonish mice category. Left over from last year, now they'll get a second chance.

Onto the squeaky cart go all these things, plus a pile of light-as-a-feather prewrapped prebow-tied gifts that contain nothing, are meant only as decorations.

By the end of the afternoon, the store is downright festive. No giant inflatable snowmen, just some nice seasonal touches. Janet doesn't like to overdo it. And, this year, who would want to?

Katrina comes in just in time to help me put out the boxes of cards. There are styles for Christmas and Hanukkah, and a couple to be sent by your business to your most valued customers.

"Hey, girlie," she asks, "where should we put these?" and I think she means the business ones but she has another box that was behind the counter. I see they're the 9-11 ones. They'd arrived with the individual Christmas cards that, like those for Mother's Day and Thanksgiving, are displayed on one of the spinnable racks. There are half a dozen styles, with one theme: patriotism. The flag, another flag, lots of red-white-and-blue designs. They are blank inside (I guess not even professional greeting-card writers know what to say inside these), so I'd been planning to put them up with their other blank relatives. But they didn't look right, a sad Statue of Liberty next to the jumping lemurs. So I'd stuck the box back behind the counter.

I still don't know where they belong. Katrina goes to the Blue Mountain rack to check if there's any room. I ring up a customer who's buying a big fat travel guide to Hawaii. It's a cheery destination, and it's great to see that somebody wants to venture farther than from home to work, and back. Fear of terrorism has spawned a general reluctance to travel. But here's somebody headed all the way to Hawaii. He asks if I could wrap the book and I offer the current choices: Birthday, All-Occasion, Wedding, Hanukkah, Christmas. He asks for Christmas and then he tells me that his next stop is Emerald City, and I know he's not headed for Oz. Emerald City Travel and my own personal travel agent, Julie Dias, are located right downstairs. As are this man's tickets to Hawaii.

"That's what I'm going to give my wife," he says, and, like the rekindling pilot, here's another guy asking, "Do you think she'll like it?"

This very soap-opera-type gift is not rare during the holiday season, I am surprised to find out, and, according to my stints at the cash register, is practiced solely by men. I only find out what they are doing because they want the travel guides wrapped. I don't mean to generalize, but 99 percent of all wrapping is done for males. If a woman mentions that this hazelnut candle is a gift, and you offer to wrap it, she'll decline, with a "No thanks, I'll do that myself" or "I have paper picked out" or "I made the paper and printed it myself and it's drying at home." Though wrapping is free, men would gladly hand over another airline ticket simply to skip the chore. So we've started to stock gift bags, and they hang within pointing distance. Even so, if you point them out—tell a man who's buying that all he has to do is go over there and take down one of the bags and shove his Fodor's inside—you get the strangest look.

Another big item this month literally is big. Coffee-table books jammed with photos of gardens, movie stars, athletes, beaches like that couple will visit in Hawaii. *The Sopranos* coffee-table book isn't as popular as you'd think. *How I Play Golf* by Tiger Woods is. The 9-11 books continue to roll in, and, just as quickly, out. I haven't wrapped any of these, but because of the season I figure some of them have to be gifts. I try to imagine one sitting beneath a tree, between a five-pack of Jockey for Her and a Salad Shooter.

We already have the gift of a new helper, because the season draws crowds—including the occasional celebrity. As Janet says, you never know who you'll meet at the bookstore. Famous customers have included entertainers Joan Rivers and David Birney, and Olympians Torville and Dean, and Kristi Yamaguchi. Also Robin Williams, who has the same birthday as Janet, but she was out when he was in. And Kenny Rogers, who was introduced to a seven-year-old Christina. Said her mother, "Christina, I'd like you to meet Mr. Rogers." Said Christina, "That's not Mr. Rogers!"

One day at the start of winter, in walks Jane Kaufman, with whom I worked during my last few years at the Union-News' bureau in my town. She was now an editor in the newspaper's main building, down the street from Tower Square.

She asks what I'm doing there, and I tell her—and that we need help for the holidays. Soon, for a few hours before her shift begins at four P.M., Jane is behind the counter, receiving, giving, fitting right in.

Hers is a trial-by-Christmas countdown. Stuff is flying. Stuff, and books, of course, large and small. The tiny tomes are big sellers and I keep watch over a particular one, the $9.99 *Erin Go Bark!* Husband and wife John O'Neill and Kim Levin traveled Ireland as Levin photographed many of the dogs that are part of that country's landscape. The couple paired the simple black-and-white shots with new takes on old sayings. "May the wind be always at your back" is given the canine-related twist of "May your coat stay shiny, your nose stay cold, and the sidewalk stay soft." I'd seen *Erin Go Bark!* in a store I can't remember during the July tour that is now but a memory, ordered a few on my return, and stacked them at the counter, where the fuzz faces have proved winning.

The new year has nosed into the store, via almanacs, atlases, and calendars. Pat has cleared some space on the side of the magazine shelves that faces the table at which we hold signings and stacked the calendars that were ordered back in a warmer season. At the CVS I buy half a dozen plastic milk crates for a couple of bucks each and set those on the signing table, which is a long rectangle and very sturdy. I sort through pets, artwork, humor, and sports, and assign each a box. To designate this as Calendar Central, I take the pages of an old desk calendar and paint the C and the A and the L and the E and the N and so on in bright blue and green paint, each letter on a separate sheet that is clothespinned to a cord and strung from the ceiling. You can't miss the word, and customers don't either. Soon they are flipping through the crates, deciding between Harley-Davidson, Dilbert, Antiques Road Show, Black History, and The Hockey Hall of Fame.

Across from Janet's side of the counter, next to the boxed Christmas cards, there's a snowdrift of secular Christmassy books for kids. Golden Book editions of *Rudolph*, the fat, chewable cardboard *Cheerios Christmas Play Book* and its cousin, *My First Christmas Board Book*. There's an *I Spy* book with items so well hidden in its colorful photographs of Christmas flotsam you could go batty trying to pick them out. And *Dream Snow,* a favorite by local author and illustrator Eric Carle, around whose work and career an entire museum is being built over in Amherst. Another popular choice, *The Night before Christmas,* as illustrated by Ruth Sanderson out in her Ware studio. And *Polar Express* in gift-box form that contains Chris Van Allsburg's 1985 Caldecott Award–winning book and a CD on which Liam Neeson reads the story of a magical nighttime train journey to the North Pole. Barry Moser moves again as people seek spiritual gifts. I place him next to *Christmas Soup for the Soul: A Christmas Treasury*, and a board book that tells the Christmas story, and I'm wondering who would let their baby chew on the Three Wise Men. *The Christmas Box* is wrapped dozens of times, as is *The Christmas Wish, The Christmas Shoes,* and *The Christmas Letter.* Janet stocks stacks of *Christmas on Jane Street,* which tells of a country family that sells trees on Manhattan's Jane Street each December. And *Stranger in the Woods,* in which photographs narrate the story of a snowman who appears in a forest, and the animals who meet him.

I'm not exaggerating when I say the store is transformed for this one month. It may not be located in the same crowded, bustling downtown my mother knew in her youth, but for thirty days or so, it's a version of that. Beginning with the city's annual day-after-Thanksgiving parade of helium characters that are like the little brothers of those who floated the day before in New York City, sales take a definite upswing. Parents escort Kaeylah and Sumner to Tower Square's Christmas Village, a rather impressive castle-type building erected on the first floor, at specified hours home to Santa himself. Seasonal tunes play from the overhead speakers. Bins marked for local food pantries are filled to overflowing with cans of tuna, and many, many packs of ramen. People line the counter at Hannoush as I take the escalator past the bins and the castle and up to Edwards, where queues have formed at the register. Arms are laden with actual piles of merchandise, and when I throw off my coat and hop into the fray, I feel a great buzz from having to enter so many ISBNs onto the cash register's ten-line computer screen that it must hop to a fresh one. Janet has stolen a display table for use as a wrapping station, but she also directs shoppers downstairs, where the mall has opened an empty store to a charity that, for a donation, will Martha-Stewart-up gifts of any size.

I fully realize that the money I'm being handed is not going into the drawer of my own cash register or anywhere near my own pocket. So it might seem odd that I get such a kick from seeing the sales soar. The reason is simply knowing that, on this day, Edwards—Janet—is making some money. In this world where "I love" and "boss" are used in the same sentence only when "the thought of kicking the ass of my" is inserted in the gap, I easily insert only the word "my." Because I love my boss. As I do all these women here in this slim space behind the counter, where they've made me so welcome and where right now Janet and Flo and Pat and Katrina and Jane and Christina are weaving around me to hunt for a book or wrap a Jungle Bowling or ring up another *Clifford's Christmas* and a box calendar—that is, when they're not asking customers the question that in the past nine months they've asked me so many times over—"How can I help you?"—and then went on to do just that.

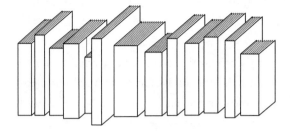

THERE'S A HANGOVER FEELING TO THE START
of this month. This new year.

Calm after clatter.

But some of that's welcome. December was a mad-
house. And that's a nice problem to have had at a small,
family owned independent bookstore in a half-vacant urban mall. On at least one day, six times the normal amount
of sales was made. We ran out of stock. Of wrapping paper. Of willpower, diving into the cookies, chocolates, and
other edible gifts proffered by the regulars.

Down comes the greenery, the bows, the fake horns of
the type you see foxhunters blowing to alert the hounds.
Up goes the 50 percent–off sign that marks the remaining
holiday books and cards. Out come the fitness books so you
can work off all you've gained. The how-to's for quitting

smoking and drinking and anger and overspending and all those other things that you have resolved to stop. At the counter, there's more hard reality: it's time for inventory.

When I got my first royalty statement, I tried to make sense of the columns and totals sent each April and September by my publisher as an accounting of books sold and books that remain available. Again, I am horrible with numbers. But making less sense to me were the words at the bottom of the first page: "Held in reserve against returns."

"Huh?"

That's when I learned how bookstores work, what very strange creatures they are in the retail world. If their merchandise does not sell, it can be returned for credit. Imagine your local grocer calling Chef Boy-Ar-Dee and explaining, "Look—nobody really was too interested in these five thousand cans of Spaghettios. Expect them in the morning mail."

The inability to return merchandise is the reason for those 75 percent–off racks in almost every other kind of store. A product, say, solar-heated underwear, is a flop. It's time to chop the price, so some money can be made. After all, the manufacturer isn't going to take back the shipment. With books, it's an entirely different story. If a book about, say, the inventor of solar-heated underwear, is neglected by readers, a bookstore can box it—and any other retail duds—and send it back to the publisher, freeing it up for any stores that are indeed moving that title. If sales are slow, or nil, the book magically transforms into a re-maindered item and is sent out to a Hawley-Cooke or Re-mains to Be Seen, where people might be a lot more willing to pay the new and improved bargain table's $5.99 price. They might not care anything about the subject. They just know they're saving eighteen bucks!

There is another option, one I didn't want to mention earlier. But this is a fitting place, as I talk about the dark, secret underbelly of the book world. In what I promise will be the final time, I'll use my meat-wrapping job as a com-parison. Finding out what happens to some unsold books is sort of like that first day on the job, when I'd donned the requisite lab coat and hair net and was led into the walk-in cooler. From hooks attached to a track suspended from the ceiling hung halves of cows, and entire sheep shapes and some other four-legged former occupants of the verses to "Old MacDonald"—not one with hair or skin or head.

Those steers grazing placidly at that quaint farm up the road, those neglected copies of *Crafting with Asbestos?* Both end up in conditions that you'd rather not.

"Shredded," Flo tells me. "They get shredded."

I cringe.

As she tells me this, Flo's stripping. Which, like dump, is not what it sounds.

What she's doing is tearing the covers off mass-market paperbacks. Those covers will be rubber banded and sent back to the publisher, and in this way the books will be considered returned. Though Flo carefully bubble wraps for return the unsold hardcover Teddy Roosevelt bio *Theo-*

dore Rex upon arrival of the paperback version, she doesn't return the mass-market books. Why should the publisher be bothered with disposing of such an inexpensive item. It's up to Flo to put them out with the recycling. They cannot be given away, or re-sold, per that note on the first page of any of these types of books, warning you that the sale of coverless books is illegal.

The stripping sound is obscene, a precursor to a mass book burning. But it's the only way the store can be credited for these copies. In the back room, I find something else to do. And I'm hoping I won't be asked to do inventory, which is like deciding which of the pets in the pound should be euthanized. Nobody's wanted to adopt the literary equivalent of Spot and Buster, so they'll have to go. It's easy for me to anthropomorphize books, if that's what I'm doing. Because I see them as creations that live and breathe. As did—or still do—their makers. Some are simply such great books that I take it personally when those I ordered for the store fail to get the proper attention. Claire Keegan's stunning debut short story collection, *Antarctica,* unfortunately fell into that category. Over in California, it was the *Los Angeles Times*'s Book of the Year. Over in Tower Square, I couldn't get anyone to take it home. I admit to checking the to-be-returned stacks near Flo's computer and sneaking back to the shelf a few books that I really think will sell if only the right person comes in. Or, as many times, just buying the thing myself. I can only imagine how many mouths I'd have to feed if I worked at an actual pound.

Pat and Flo are tougher. And they've been doing inventory a long time, progressing around the store section by section, book by book, looking up each title on a printout.

"First you look to see when the book came in," Pat explains. "Then you check to see when's the last time it sold. If it's six or more months and there's two on the shelf, I'll pull one. If there are three, I'll pull two. I'll leave something there unless the book is a year old. Then I'll pull it off."

Even though milk-bottle-like expiration dates aren't stamped on the covers, books have them, I guess. A shelf life that takes into account not only time, but also popularity.

By the time Flo and Pat have inventoried the entire store, which takes maybe three or four months, it's time to start again. Right now, they're in the Native American section, researching the sales of those books, which are Pat's specialty. She's a Penobscot, and the Penobscot are part of the Abenaki Nation that once reached from New Hampshire north to Canada and west to the Great Lakes. Finding new sources of books dealing with Native American culture is important to her.

"I think we have something to say," Pat tells me. "It's a minority community that is sort of in limbo. Nobody knows we're here, and I would like to expand that section and make people aware that Native American people contribute to this country more than just casinos."

I received a hint of those cultural riches back in May, when I connected with the deer. Pat tapped into her beliefs and, via U.S. mail, blessed me with an important gift. The deer, she told me, is now my totem animal. It appeared in my life for a reason. Her copy of a book on totem animals said that, among other wonderfully pertinent qualities, deer teach us to find the gentleness of spirit that heals all wounds. To remind me of my link to this animal, and to its qualities and lessons, she sent me a small figurine of two resting deer. Though I have to say I think first of Pat when I look at them each morning, and feel just as grateful for her appearance in my story.

As she does for Native American, Pat reads the catalogs for Fantasy, knows what should be ordered, and says that while inventorying she roots for the titles she's ordered and feels disappointed when something she believes is a winner doesn't get sold. Everyone on the staff shares that feeling with their favorites. So we sneak a peek at our individual recommendation tables to see what's moving. I know I glance over to see if anyone's plucked a book from my batch, among them *Then She Found Me, The Children of Strangers, She's Come Undone, Uphill Walkers, The Pilot's Wife, Blue Italian, Ruby's Café, Going with the Grain, Writing from the Heart, Pears on a Willow Tree, Blind Side of the Heart, Revere Beach Elegy, Frontera Street, House.* If one is missing, you hope it exited only after making a stop at the counter. Each item in the inventory contains a bit of modern magic that alerts sensors at the door that unpaid merchandise is being carried out. They go WWHHHHEEEEP! and are very embarrassing to those who have paid for an item that was not demagnetized properly at the cash register and so tripped the alarm. The sensors are there because people come into Edwards for reasons other than to browse or read or buy or say hi to Mother. Janet has eyes like the Bionic Woman. Especially when somebody's doing something wrong. She'll only look as if she's doing her banking via phone, but she'll suddenly whisper, "That person just took something" and drop her pen and run around the counter and toward the door, and retrieve the item from the culprit, who usually surrenders it, with a "How'd that get in my pants?"

I like to think the best of people. I don't like to interrupt them, either. I have been known to ask browsers if they need help, but sometimes even that innocuous and pretty much expected retail question strikes some weird fear in the hearts of shoppers and chases them right out the door. Janet seems to know which customers to assist and which to just plain watch. She'll roam the store, circle a set of shelves, in some cases she'll outright stare.

I've seen evidence that not everybody who walks through the door is Dudley-Do-Right honest. They take things. They take wedding cards and they take ankle bracelets and they take lemon votives and they take magazines about personal computers. As you shift a shelf of merchandise you might find a bar code ripped from the dust jacket of *Desecration: Antichrist Takes the Throne* because whoever took it thought that the bar code was what might alert the sensors. You might spot it on the floor near the freebie papers. The *Valley Advocate,* the area's alternative newspaper and the *Union-News*'s only print competition. Or near the more family-ish regional freebies. The *Journal,* the *Reminder, Bravo, Women's Times.* Thieving patrons have been known to use the freebies to wrap around merchandise that is not free. Or you might find they've taken the book but left the dust jacket on the shelf, to make it look like the pages remain. Or, you might just re-alize there was a pile of books there a second ago and now it's gone. Which causes me to note that the theft of five hardcover copies of Marie Osmond's autobiography, *Behind the Smile: My Journey out of Postpartum Depression*, remains unsolved.

Whether aromatherapy freaks, jewelry-a-olics, or just a little bit country, a little bit rock 'n' roll, thieves are the exception. Witness the pile of money lying on the counter all day. It's the coins with which people pay for their papers. There's no sign explaining. If there's no one at the counter to take your 50 or 75¢, feel free to leave it. The drop-off was Janet's idea, an honor system she instituted shortly after coming to Edwards.

"When I worked in the city, on the corner of Madison Avenue and Forty-second Street was one guy I wouldn't recognize if I saw him," she tells me. "His back was always to the public as he was stocking shelves. He had a cigar box on the top of a stack of newspapers, and people would throw money in, take change. I said to my mother 'If they can do it on Forty-second Street, we can do it on Main Street in Springfield.' This store is a neighborhood, in some sense."

Newcomers are swift to point out the $2.50 or so that might be sitting there. "Somebody left some money here," they say with such concern that you might think it's a $50-dollar bill rather than 50 cents. When you tell them it's just newspaper money, they give you a weird look. "People leave it—for newspapers," you explain.

"In this day and age?!"

* * *

Should we have any real problems, we need only dial a phone number and be rescued by Javish.

I wish there were photos in this book so I could show you Javish, a twenty-six-year-old native of Puerto Rico who served from 1996 to 1999 in the U.S. Marine Corps' First Battalion, Eighth Marines, officially known as the Foul Weather Warriors and unofficially as Uncle Jimmy's Gun Club, an affectionate jab at the battalion commander. He participated in Operation Joint Guard in Bosnia, Operation Silver Wake in Albania, and Operation Guardian Retrieval in Zaire, and has spent time in Panama, Okinawa, and Korea. He now does the same in Tower Square, where he is a security guard, despite the fact that he could be on Comedy Central with a totally different stand-up routine nightly.

No photo, so imagine Javish, trim buzz cut, cheeky expression as he looks at you through Clark Kent glasses and removes a notepad from the shirt pocket of his black-and-white Cosigna uniform. So he can show you—and me—cartoon drawings.

Javish has many stories he'd like to tell, much advice to give. For instance, he guarantees that my books would be best sellers if I included car chases and great amounts of weaponry. Then his walkie-talkie buzzes and he's off to answer a call in another part of the building, rushing past the gang of women in search of wedding books. June is the traditional month for that occasion, but Christmas is usually the start, Janet explains, after directing them to

Poetry/Reference/Drama, where they compare planners and select the *Working Woman's Wedding Planner*, big and shiny, with wide plastic spirals making up the spine. Last month, diamonds were popular Christmas gifts. Probably had been wrapped along with a travel guide about and airline tickets to Bermuda. Because one of the women asks the kind of question you have to run off and write down: "Do you have a book on how to speak Bermudian?"

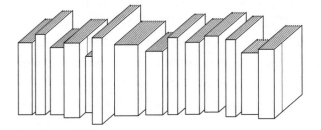

I have found the real secret to creating a best seller.

Just seal it in plastic and slap on a warning label.

Such as that found on *Seduction: The Art of the Female Orgasm.*

You could title your book *Lumpy the Clam* and, I believe, if you wrapped it in plastic and applied a label reading "For Adults Only," *Lumpy* would sell millions.

I believe this because I have been observing the sales of *Seduction* since its arrival in the store last month. Granted, it was written by *Sex and the City* star Kim Cattrall, whose character regularly has relations with approximately the entire city. So her name on the cover doesn't hurt the book's chances. Also on there are the names of Mark Levinson, her jazz-playing now-ex-husband, and Fritz Drury, illustrator whose pencil is responsible for the plastic and sticker, but who reads farther than Cattrall? Yet I don't hear people exclaiming "Kim Cattrall!" when they pick up this book. I hear them exclaim, "It's sealed in plastic!" "It's For Adults Only!" Ring up another sale.

Seduction makes it onto the *New York Times* best seller list, which, at Edwards, means it automatically is priced at 20 percent off, making it an even better seller.

Timely release dates don't hurt. You'd have to release *Lumpy* around the hubbub of National Bivalve Day, or something to that effect. Kim had the foresight to plan her book's launch for the big hot holiday of Valentine's Day. Which is why she's front and center these days.

As is the young woman waving a copy of *101 Nights of Grrreat Sex: Secret Sealed Seductions for Fun-Loving Couples*, written by Laura Corn, who probably isn't a farmer.

Another key to literary success:

Sealed pages.

That's the state of the pages in *101 Nights*. They're glued shut. The activities proposed inside each set are a surprise, but the exteriors do bear symbols indicating whether what you're about to do will call for money, going out, or, in some cases, being certain everyone else in the house has gone out.

Oddly, the only book that caused a ruckus in my first year at Edwards was a paper doll book featuring Pope John Paul II. It's one in a series that features celebrities past and present, and it included a pop-out pope in white, floor-length everyday wear to be dressed in authentically detailed garb for several events on the church calendar. I entered the store one day to see the JPII missing from his space between Ronald and Nancy Reagan and Carmen Miranda.

"Hey! You sold the pope!"

Oh it is a kick to see that one of your choices has sold.

"I put him out back," Janet said, frowning. "One man was very upset, said it was irreverent. He made a scene."

When it comes to racey merchandise at Edwards, there are a few items other than a fully clothed papal paper doll about which to squawk. But not tons. When I asked Janet about the absence of the usual "adult" publications that you might want to handle with tongs but that certainly would bring in gobs of income, she answered as quickly and clearly and unwaveringly as I should have back at that scholarship interview:

"That's easy. We are a family. Three generations with lots of good books and magazines to recommend. I always think of us as not just family owned and operated, but family friendly, also. There are lots of magazine stands you can go to for adult magazines. That just isn't our mission."

Anyway, there's already enough in this store that's often too adult. As in too-real and too-harsh and too-cruel reality. As in the photos of *Wall Street Journal* reporter Daniel Pearl that were printed in each of the newspapers the day after his January 23 kidnapping in Pakistan.

Pearl once wrote for the Springfield Newspapers, where I spent most of my reporting career. Back then he worked from the now-defunct Berkshire Bureau an hour from Springfield, so our paths never crossed. But since his kidnapping, I'd followed the story. And cringed at the photos of him on subsequent front pages, his head bowed as someone else's two hands gripped a gun angled toward the reporter who was suddenly a prisoner.

When he was abducted in Karachi, Pearl was retracing the steps of "shoe bomber" Richard Reid and hoping to meet with militant extremists. There was no word on his fate until he was confirmed dead on February 21. After which more photos, and some very gruesome details about his killing, went page one. From behind the counter I looked over to the newspaper shelves, where Pearl's face took up the front of the tabloids.

It was the man in the sinking plane all over again. I felt horrible for his family, for his wife, for their unborn child, and for Jane. She'd known him when they both were reporters in the Berkshires. She's now being interviewed. Before she starts her shift at the paper, Jane puts in a few hours at the store, and must walk past the face of her friend printed again and again on all those front pages.

To quote British folk-rock bard Billy Bragg, "Valentine's Day is over." In a lot of ways. Nationwide, clouds of hate are ever-thickening. I plop the few remaining *Seduction*s onto the squeaky cart and for a new display harvest titles that might help somebody cope with the person in the next cubicle, house, town, state, country. Because that's how it starts. At least that's how it starts in the Blue Mountain of my brain, from which Rodney King cries out, "Can't we all just get along?" If you can learn to coexist with the overenthusiastic Amway salesman who shares your bus stop, a ripple might begin. Or so we can hope. With that as the goal, the books that will now greet you as you enter the store: *Dealing with Difficult People, How to Deal with Difficult People, Dealing with People You Can't Stand*. And, because all this should start early, the kids' $3.99 *Getting Along with Others: A Workbook*. I add one more title, fresh from an Ingram box. Just released this month and written in the wake of 9-11 is *Bad Stuff in the News: A Guide to Handling the Headlines,* in which "God Squad" columnists and commentators Rabbi Marc Gellman and Monsignor Thomas Hartman counsel kids in grades six through ten on facts of life—these particular ones being terrorism, school violence, natural disasters, hatred, racism, bad sportsmanship, and physical, sexual, and emotional abuse. Above the table hangs the red paper heart that had floated over the books on love. I leave it in place.

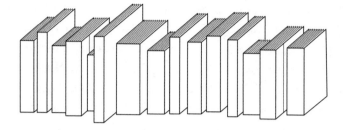

TO THE LEFT OF JANET'S COMPUTER, JUST PAST
the tall stack of catalogs and bills and letters, almost in
front of the end of the counter that Pat likes to try to keep
clear for her work, is the paper bag on which is written a
single all-capitals word:

TEETH.

The labeling is to help you locate them upon the return of the man who left on the counter his pair of dentures.

"Yes, teeth," Pat assures me. "Usually it's keys, or a cell
phone, sunglasses, sometimes a purse. Today it was teeth."
She gives me a "What can you do?" sort of shrug and turns
to make change for a guy giving her a twenty for a fifty-
cent paper as a lot of people tend to do first thing in the
morning.

Janet was the brave one, picking up the teeth with a plastic-bag-encased hand and then double bagging them in a paper sack meant for greeting cards or small paperbacks, longing for the mouth they call home.

That mouth actually is a familiar one. A guy who's in often enough, who is a tad peculiar for living in his own little world but who never before left behind any body parts. We have no information on his name, no phone number. We'll just have to wait until the day he sits down for a steak and realizes something's amiss.

Forgotten teeth are a first for me, here at the start of my twelfth month working at Edwards. Though Christiane Northrop's *The Wisdom of Menopause: Creating Physical and Emotional Health and Healing during the Change* landed at Edwards the same month I did, and has been a titanic best seller ever since, I'm talking about a different type of change. Time is so healing that when the insurance companies learn how to charge for it we're all going to be in trouble. I have a space of twelve months between me and that lost, lethargic, lumpy-clam state and where I am now is like looking back from the stern of a boat and seeing the coastline of a country in which you had a really rotten vacation getting smaller by each turn of the propeller. But I think the big reason I feel so much more stable is due to how I spent that twelve months. I might still be curled up in my chair if it weren't for the ejection seat that Janet's year-ago phone call proved to be. Had my doctor scrawled on a prescription pad: "Four and a half hours selling books, 2X week," would I have listened? Like many of the wondrous and awful things that have shaped my life, the job fell from the sky, a 3,500-square-foot version of Dorothy's farmhouse that landed at the start of a road I didn't feel I had the energy to walk without a daily afternoon nap. For Dorothy, that journey was the only way home. For me, walking out the door of my house and getting into my car and driving into the big, unpredictable world was similar. I felt far from the familiar me who once lived in my skin. That's where I wanted to get back to. And that's what I wrote about while I was sick. In daily entries kept during the six and a half weeks of radiation, pages I ultimately was encouraged to send to my agent, that caught the interest of a publishing house, and that, in hardcover book form, on a sparkling day this very month, were rolled through the door of Edwards by the UPS man.

Flo signed for them and the next chance she got took the box out back to inventory, and then returned to her computer to receive.

And when I arrived that afternoon, there was much hoopla and waving about of the new book and I yelled, "Time's up!" to whichever *New York Times* best seller had sold so well that copies of it were nearly extinct and I refilled its dump with copies of my new book.

You can do that sort of thing when you work in a bookstore, which is what I'm doing exactly one year after Janet's phone call.

Across from the hijacked dump is this year's St. Patrick's Day display, which takes up one green-clothed table. The glass shelves behind it have been given over to National Poetry Month, which is in April but, being very much on the ball, I have had that exhibit up for a few weeks already. I've even blurred the displays, including poetry in each. On the front table is a copy of *The Ballyconnell Colours* by Irish poet/author/autobiographer/playwright/all-around creative type Dermot Healy. The very last page of the book is the very last page of the title poem, in which Healy, as is usually the case with poets, has to be talking about something big and deep and cosmic, but on that very last page are nothing but the final five lines, which I realize could double as a description of how I got to the place I now stand:

> *The unyielding stars,*
> *And the white seal pup on the rocks*
> *Thrown up here,*
> *Like myself,*
>
> *In a storm.*

I step through the doors of the store and stand over by the escalator to check how the hijacked dump looks from the view of the passerby. It's even with the entryway, so there's little chance you'll miss it, unless you're looking elsewhere, as I'm doing right now, to the center of the store where a collegiate-type young man at the counter is asking if there are any jobs available. I hear Janet say, "Sorry, we're a family business. We only hire family." Thing is, she's not blowing him off. She means the family thing. Not in some kind of overly familiar cultish way. It's just that when fate delivers you to a place where you are made welcome, a version of family member is what you can become. Due both to the size of place—the limited square footage behind the counter being one factor—and to simply the fact that those who were delivered there before you regularly pack acceptance and compassion into the pockets of their Ann Taylor blazers, their Navajo-print coats, their graffitied backpacks, their big black handbags, and their *Baywatch* Barbie lunch bags.

I walk away from the store to the other side of hall, just in front of the enormous, maybe fifteen-foot-long photograph, of downtown Springfield. The Connecticut River spanned by the Memorial Bridge and its strange ornamental poles topped with spikey balls that when I was a kid and even now look like something a giant would hurl. Then the brick and concrete shore that grew from that 1660s fort. I sit on the bench at the foot of the photograph and look across the escalator gap to the bookstore. It's shining. An effect you could say is caused by the darkness of the adjacent retail spaces. I could say that, too. Except I know better.

Because I sell books now.

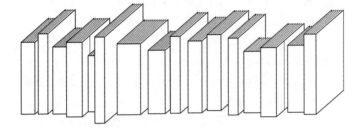

THE SPRING THIS BOOK WILL BE PUBLISHED, I will conclude my third year at Edwards Books.

I'm writing this chapter the October before, so I actually am taking a chance that I still will be working there. But, really, I'm not. It's a pretty good bet that I'll continue to have something to do with the store even if I do hit the literary big time and move to an Irish beach dotted with storm-tossed seal pups looking around and asking, "Where the hell am I?" I'll know where they are, so I'll inform them. Because that's what you sometimes need when you find yourself in an unfamiliar beach, country, world. Somebody to say, "You're with me and you're fine and you're loved."

Right now (I'm stopping here to knock wood), that is my very status.

As for more detailed updates:

Flo's seventy-nine now but she's not going anywhere ("Where would I go?").

And neither is Janet. (Asks same question.)

Pat's still opening the store five days a week, Katrina's still closing it on an as-needed basis. (She's also working at the newspaper, taking classified ads and obituaries by day, and by night selling a line of gourmet food mixes at home parties.) Jane is still at the paper, but not often at the bookstore because she's currently house-sitting in a town far in the opposite direction. We root for her next residence to be a little more Edwards-convenient.

Christina is loving being a freshman up the street at the High School of Commerce. As for her own dreams, right now they include a career as a lawyer or an actress.

"Nothing book related?"

"Well," Christina starts, "I have thought about being a writer. In the sixth grade especially I had lots of creative writing assignments and I got A's. But I don't know about that for the rest of my life. Right now, all the options are open."

As of this writing, television service to Christina's home has not been resumed; she and Janet nightly continue to devour books at lightning speed. Fiction and non.

One of the hottest recently released nons was Hillary Clinton's autobiography, which proved so instantly popular that we had to take orders. I made a poster announcing that fact and decorated it with a collage of Hill and Bill and Rudy Giuliani and their accompanying cartoon-balloon comments—Rudy was saying, "I read it!" and Hill, in a comment from her promotional tour, was noting, "I love Bill's hands." The collage caused a ruckus among some shoppers; perhaps one of them the pope doll protester. As for those exiled paper papal dolls, I ended up buying them to send as a Christmas gift to an extremely conservative priest-friend, who thought they were simply delightful.

A Novel Idea closed its doors in May 2003, shortly after the town got its first megasupermarket, which contains a wide aisle lined with the latest books.

My town still has a bookmobile, and my town's library, as of this writing, has a cupola on the soon-to-be-completed expansion and renovation project.

My town also still has a smutty bookstore.

Over at the library, the Book Loft continues to roar with business.

Eric Carle has his own museum, just north of there, in Amherst.

The Windows on the World wine book is now in its fourth edition, despite the restaurant being long gone.

Marianne Pearl gave birth to Adam, wrote *Mighty Heart: The Life and Death of Daniel Pearl,* and is living in New York when not out publicizing the book.

War began. A whole lot of people got killed. War ended. A whole lot of people still are getting killed.

More than a few Edwards customers place special orders for *The Individual's Guide for Understanding and Surviving Terrorism* and *Surviving Terrorism,* penned in 2002 by the U.S. Marine Corps. They also want *How to Understand, Anticipate and Respond to Terrorist Attacks,* by Rainer Stahlberg, which was published just last summer. Back in another world—1998 to be specific—Stahlberg authored the relatively innocent *The Complete Book of Survival: How to Protect Yourself against Revolution, Riots, Hurricanes, Famines and Other Natural and Man-Made Disasters.* We field the occasional query about the 30,007-page CD-ROM of *21st Century Complete Guide to Bioterrorism, Biological and Chemical Weapons, Germs and Germ Warfare, Nuclear and Radiation Terrorism — Military Manuals and Federal Documents with Practical Emergency Plans, Protective Measures, Medical Treatment and Survival Information*, released by the U.S. government on September 30, 2001.

Greeting cards are still being purchased to send overseas. There still isn't an easy answer for those seeking the right words to put inside.

The escalator continues to break on a whim, and Tower Square has closed our employee bathroom "down the hall," necessitating fast walks much farther down the hall to another facility.

The quarters left on the counter remain untouched.

I have renamed the dungeon "The Gold Mine." There is just too much fantastic stuff down there. More, we find out, since Flo and I have started monthly treks to sort through and haul upstairs.

As for salable "stuff," the inventory has expanded. A signing at a Polish festival in New York State in fall 2002 led me to meet an importer of Polish amber and an importer of *Boleslawiec* Polish pottery. Both lines have been selling like *goracy ciastki*.

The Judge was the subject of an embarrassing typo but he handled with grace the ensuing jokes. A photographer from the *Sunday Republican* had visited the store to photograph readers for its "What They're Reading" feature, and the Judge's smiling face appeared above a quote that told he was currently reading a World War II novel titled *The Children's War*. "It's the longest book I ever read. It's 110 pages."

Problem was, *The Children's War* is 1,100 pages.

And in what was not a typo, the *Union-News* was renamed *The Republican*.

The Odyssey Bookshop is celebrating its fortieth anniversary.

Chicopee's Fairfield Mall, once home to The First Edition, and Edwards Books' original location, was knocked down. In its place is a fenced-in mall-shaped heap of dirt. To the left of that, a sparkling new Home Depot.

Erin Go Bark! continues to be a big seller. In the same category is *Quit*, a $5.99 book shaped like a pack of cigarettes, bearing a Marlboro-ian red-and-white color scheme and filled with inspiration and information for snuffing the habit. I spotted *Quit* at the Brookline Booksmith in October 2001 and over the next year we sold scores. The added bonus to this hit is that it's actually helping somebody.

After helping herself, *Sex for One* author Betty Dodson went on to write *Orgasms for Two*. Pat and I are taking bets on what will be her third title.

All *Sopranos* books were duds in this store—except for the 2002 *A Goomba's Guide to Life* by Steven R. Schirripa, who plays Uncle Junior's gofer, Bobby Bacala. Just as we can credit the Judge for the record sales of *Ghost Soldiers,* we can give credit for the Goomba's modest local popularity to the word spread by Howie Munson, owner of the food court's french fry mecca, Tower Grill, and Schirripa's fellow graduate of the Class of 1975 at Lafayette High in New York's Bensonhurst.

And speaking of *Ghost Soldiers,* it's out in paperback now, and it's usually just out. It's still a store favorite and is still on my to-read list so I can't join in the raving, but its dump space now is occupied by Laura Hillenbrand's *Seabiscuit.* The book, not the horse, but two dumps were sent by the publisher, and they're side by side so they do take up the space of a barn animal.

On the third Thursday of the month, they're slid over a bit for some real animals. Because Janet's good works continue. Every third Thursday of the month, from noon to one thirty, the store holds its Pet Project, a visit by critters from the MSPCA shelter down the street. Usually it's a cage with two or three cats or kittens and a dog who's leashed and wearing an ADOPT ME vest. The events spark interest in customers, and even if they don't adopt these very animals, the idea is in their heads to perhaps visit the shelter. In several cases, the critters who visited— including a usually hard-to-place thirteen-year-old dog— indeed went to bookstore customers' homes.

Janet has also been involved with a group of residents who've worked to persuade the city to purchase the privately held library system, a move that is related to the main library and branches possibly reopening or being open longer hours. I'm sitting in my pajamas (I wear them only at night now) watching the evening news and there she is on TV giving hell to the opposition.

Blue Mountain remains the Everest of emotional

greetings. Next to this line, as of last month, are a rack of cards bearing photos of local scenes shot by none other than Belchertown resident and nationally best-selling author Julius Lester. I might send a couple to pals Amy and Celeste, who remain in touch even though we haven't crossed paths since Stillwater. I also hear from Jamie Storer over in Ireland, whose offer of work sparked the idea that will become my fifth novel, *Becoming Finola*, in which a woman travels to Ireland, walks into a craft shop, is offered work, and begins to slip into many other aspects of the life of the women who previously held the job.

Since I wrote this, Oprah concluded her book club and then restarted it in a new incarnation, one focusing on classics and making tons of money for whoever holds the publishing rights to books by dead writers. I never got into her first club and, still breathing, I'm not eligible for the second. But that's A-OK because I recently received recognition beyond compare.

I saw Title Man at a table, and heard him say: "Songs ... from ... a ... Lead ... Lined ... Room ... Notes ... High ... and ... Low ... from ... My ... Journey ... through ... Breast ... Cancer ... and ... Radiation ... by ... Su ... Su.... Susan.... S ... Stemk ... Sheeuh."

Bradley Trevor Greive remains an impulse-buy hero. His backlist now also includes *Looking for Mr. Right, The Incredible Truth about Motherhood, The Blue Day Journal, Price-*

less: The Vanishing Beauty of a Fragile Planet, Tomorrow: Adventures in an Uncertain World, The Blue Day Notebook, and *The Blue Day Frog* (with a toy frog attached).

The pilot has yet to fly back into the store to tell us if the earrings did the rekindling trick. I can't decide whether his absence is a good thing—did everything work out perfectly and he's managing a ChickFilet somewhere in Houston just so he won't have to be away all the time? Or did she hate the earrings (on second thought, they were kinda big) or he didn't remember her earlobes were allergic to metal or that she doesn't have earlobes—whatever it was, something went wrong and she applied an industrial-strength extinguisher to whatever little smoking ember he was trying to fan, and he's never going to come back in the store because he just cannot talk about it.

"There are lots of stories waiting to circle around again," Janet tells me. "Sometimes you find out what happened and how things went. But there are a lot of stories that have yet to be told."

For the pilot, for you, for me, change is the one guaranteed story element. And should the day dawn when you look in the mirror and aren't sure who's looking back, remember the words of Flo: You can do anything you want. And remember mine: Get thee to a bookstore.

You never know what you'll find in there. Maybe a copy, as well as the feeling, of *The Unbearable Lightness of Being.* Or, as one shopper called that book, "Light-headedness."

Whatever you call it, it's enough—more than enough—to say I'm being. An existence that includes writing and walking and kayaking and gardening and spending a couple of hours a week at Edwards. Where, at the very end of last month, when Janet saw a man approaching the counter with lips pulled tight over his gums, she held up the bag with the one word written in all caps. Throughout each of the store's 3,500 square feet was heard this jubilant exclamation: "My teeth!"

Now they were back in his hands, soon to be back in his mouth, the mouth that was part of a smile that, while not the stuff of toothpaste commercials, was real and genuine and showed his astonishment over going into a small, family owned independent bookstore in a half-dark, half-closed urban mall and walking out with something he never thought he'd find there.

Which, if you leave out the detail of the dentures, is the exact same thing that happened to me.

ACKNOWLEDGMENTS

One freezing night back in February of 2003, I was walking down Boylston Street in Boston with Helene Atwan, director of Beacon Press, when she asked the question every writer wants to hear from the head of a publishing house: "So what are you going to write for us next?" I thank her for asking, and for, seven months later, enthusiastically accepting my 223-page reply. Not one page of it, I should note, would exist without the generous imprimatur of Janet Edwards, owner of Edwards Books in Springfield, Massachusetts. Love and thanks to her, and to all the other powerful women behind that bookstore's counter: Flo Edwards, Christina Giliberti, Pat Rossi, Katrina Deragon, Jane Kaufman, and Andrea Stone. Gratitude also to the staff at Beacon Press—especially Tom Hallock, Lisa Sacks, Kathy Daneman, and Katie O'Neil. And, as always, to Tommy Shea, Elinor Lipman, John Talbot, and readers everywhere.